The Military Horse

Marshall Cavendish London & New York

Edited by Sue Simmons

Published by Marshall Cavendish Publications Limited,
58 Old Compton Street, London W1V 5PA

© Marshall Cavendish Publications Limited 1976

First printing 1976

ISBN 0 85685 140 X

Printed in Great Britain by
Severn Valley Press Limited

Introduction

The role of the horse, and man's reliance on him in the theatre of war, have altered completely in view of the enormous transformations which have taken place on the battlefields of the past century. The horse is today demoted to the status of a dumb pack animal used in remote and impenetrable areas of the world where the machines of war cannot go, but this lowly rank should not reflect badly upon the proud position once held by the military horse on the field of conflict in the past.

The Military Horse recaptures the days when man's only means of rapid transit and extra strength – from the animal's earliest domestications in the valleys of the Middle East to the days of the Dark Ages when the heavy horse, equipped with the finest of accoutrements, was a deadly weapon in himself and a determining factor in European conflicts. The romance of the Age of Chivalry, when a knight's horse was also his most faithful and trusted companion, the training schools of the eighteenth century nobility and the use of the horse in guerilla warfare waged by groups as diverse as the ancient Britons, the Indians of North America and the Boers are all chronicled in these pages, together with the exploits and tactics of the far-sighted commanders who adapted the potential of the horse to the conditions of their day, from Ghengis Khan and Tamurlaine to Gustavis Adolphus and Cromwell, Washington and Napoleon.

As the horse becomes increasingly an object for our leisure hours, we should remember the spectacular role of this magnificent creature in the most aggressive of man's pursuits.

Contents

The Military Horse

For centuries man has used the horse to provide power, strength and speed to help him adapt to the exigencies of a constantly changing world. But, in no pursuit has man made more demands on the horse than in that of war. In no other capacity must the horse accept so much responsibility: to face the pounding of guns, to charge headlong into the enemy rank and file, to hear the shrieks and cries of men and horses and catch the terrifying scent of blood and yet still remain disciplined and alert to his rider's every command.

In the wild state the horse is one of nature's pacifists, living a herdic life, a herbivore whose natural defence is that of fleeing from any danger. It was thus a long path from man's first domestication of the horse to his role on the battlefields of the world.

Much is known about the evolution of the horse from archaeological discoveries throughout North America, Asia and Europe but little concrete evidence is available as to when man first learned to ride him.

It is clear that early man knew the horse well—around 30,000 BC the vague lines on the walls of cave dwellings took on a more definite shape and of all the animal subjects figured in these early attempts at art the horse seems to have been the most popular. By the New Stone Age, the drawing became more elaborate, more suggestive of magic, religious or hunting ritual. Yet there is no sign of man having contemplated riding the animal.

The experts are confusing if not confused about when and where animal husbandry first took place, but it is generally agreed that the nomad hunter on the open prairies and sweeping ridges of the steppes took the first steps in keeping and riding horses. The early nomad hunter no longer returning to last year's cave followed the herds of wild horses, cattle and deer through the length and breadth of two continents, from Western Europe to China. Their economy was still based on the simplest principles of hunting and gathering, moving house and home with the herds when these moved on in search of richer pastures and raiding them whenever their basic needs required it.

Nomadic man, hunting the wild herds of horses, would soon have caught the newly-born foal or heavily-pregnant mare. Finding himself left with an inedible youngster, the hunter could have taken him back to the tents for his own children to play with or to use in training them in the arts of hunting. From the small group of pregnant mares, he soon realized that he had, in fact, gained a real asset. What better economics than to take with you from camp to camp your food, milk, child's companion and teaching aid which needs little attention and feeds itself. So, in addition to their goats and dogs, the nomad families began to take with them a small herd of horses.

At the earliest level of the excavated township of Catal Hüyük, founded in Anatolia around 8000 BC, clay figurines of children riding what appear to be leopards or calves have been found. So, if the children of the town climbed on the backs of leopards and calves, would not his gypsy brother, in play, have jumped on the back of a young pony, giving his father the idea that travel on four legs was easier than travel on two?

From then on the horse's future was inextricably linked to that of man. By being able to harness and control the horse, man could use its speed and mobility to aid him in every aspect of life.

Simple, kind bits fashioned from bone, found along the nomad routes stretching from Ancient Britain to China, testify to the development of equipment. By 1500 BC man had discovered that training and kind treatment produced beneficial results. Kikkulis, master of the horse to the kings of Hittites, anticipated the discoveries of the eighteenth-century training schools. In his treatise chipped out on tablets of stone, he said that care must be given to the training and feeding of horses. It was he who advised his royal patrons that the animal's diet must be balanced if he was to gallop over long distances and pointed out that intelligent training of the horse made him more efficient. And it was he who counselled the use of 'kindness and co-operation' rather than force and the rule of the whip.

The superiority of some breeds was also discovered: the Arab has been used by man in all ages to improve and specialize existing stock and war was always the best possible incentive to horse breeding to ensure the swiftest and most agile horses possible. Leather armour first devised and used by the Assyrian warriors began the long development to the heavily protected horse of medieval times.

Hence man learned to use the horse, not only in the peaceful pursuits of everyday life but in the most horrific of man's activities. But as in every historical role the horse has been cast, he has served innumerable masters with courage, spirit, devotion and strength.

Right *As man's early attempts at art took on a more definite form, the horse became prominent as one of his most popular subjects. Although at first merely reflecting man's everyday existence, by the New Stone Age these drawings, such as this one at Altimira, had become more suggestive of magic, religious or hunting ritual.*

Centre right *An Assyrian mounted soldier defends himself against an enemy infantryman. Among the most efficient and innovatory people to use the horse, the Assyrians were the first to realize his potential in cavalry units.*

Far right *A Sumerian mosaic of about 2100 BC showing part of a battle and victory scene. The four wheeled cart is in fact an early chariot of a very heavy build and with solid wheels. Onagers or wild asses are being used to pull it, animals which because of difficult temperament were soon to be replaced by the horse.*

The genesis of the military horse

Throughout early history, the greatest dependence in war fell upon the infantryman or foot soldier. It was not until the last thousand years BC that the mounted horseman began to play a major part in warfare and many more centuries were to pass before disciplined cavalry was used to its full effect.

The age of the chariot

The earliest use of the horse in war appears to have been in the drawing of primitive chariots. Nomadic man had herded his horses from one area to another: civilized man, with the invention of the wheel, began to drive the horse. The development of the chariot had a major impact on the period, lifting man above the primitive warfare of club and spear and engendering not only a revolution in mobility and efficiency but also a new status symbol for the ruling class.

The Mesopotamians were the first people known to use chariots, which were of a very simple construction with solid wheels and pulled by mules. Horsedrawn chariots were apparently first used by the Hyksos, who introduced both the horse and the chariot into Egypt when they invaded about 1800 BC.

The Egyptians were quick to learn of the advantages of using these vehicles, especially on their hard level ground. When the Hyksos eventually withdrew, Egypt became a military power in her own right and in the course of her extensive conquests she not only proved the superiority of her war chariots but also improved her horse stock by cross-breeding her horses with those from the coast of Phoenicia.

The chariot became much more sophisticated during this time. It was heavier, requiring more horses to pull it and had by now acquired spoked wheels. Repairs were carefully provided; carpenters were always a part of an army on campaign. Tactics were evolving. No longer did each chariot act individually, driving into enemy ranks, but as a unit, armed with javelins and bows to countermand the growing mobility and protective armour of their opponents.

The horses pulling the chariots were probably of mixed stock but the hot-blooded Arab had already made his mark. These horses can be traced back to the period of history when Arabia was a green and fertile land. The ancient Arabs worshipped the sun, moon, and the stars, and the horse idol Ya'uk; in Southern Arabia the idol was Ya'bub (a swift horse). These horses appear on the temple walls in Egypt and in the wars of Seti and Rameses.

In the wars with the Hittites the superiority of the Egyptians was crucial. By the time of Rameses II in 1288 BC, the military strength of Egypt had declined and new waves of migrating peoples threatened her lands. Rameses, however, was determined to restore Egypt to its full extent and at the battle of Kadesh, although completely outmanoeuvred by the Hittite leaders, he managed to win the day, largely by the superiority of his force of charioteers, armed with their compact long-range bows.

However, Egypt then went into a slow decline, threatened by the Assyrians, an aggressive and

Above *As the Egyptians developed the chariot, it became a sign of status— only the Pharaohs and the richest aristocrats using them for hunting and war purposes.*

Right *Assurbanipal's cavalry charging the enemy archers. The Assyrian mounted warriors are fighting with only the most rudimentary equipment and with little protection for man or horse, although later a simple form of armour was devised using thick leather pieces.*

vigorous people from the north. The chariot played a broad role in the Assyrian battle strategy, and they were the first to develop a separate cavalry arm. Armed with spears and bows, the soldiers would ride in twos, one rider to hold the horses and to protect the other rider with a large shield, who released his arrows at the enemy.

The chariot retained its importance and became heavier, carrying up to four or five soldiers into battle. However, its use was largely determined by terrain. It was difficult to drive such a heavy vehicle up or down slopes, a factor which played a large part in its decline. The chariot eventually lost its military effectiveness and was relegated to use for racing only.

The availability of quality horses also determined the use of chariots. For a long period after their settlement in Canaan, the Hebrews did not use the chariot. Their hilly terrain and hostility to the Egyptians, the main suppliers of horses, proved almost insuperable handicaps.

The Greek Empire

The earliest Greek representation of the horse dates only from about 1600 BC, and riding appears not to have been practised by the Greeks before 500 BC. From that time, however, we hear of the growing importance of cavalry units in northern Greece. Throughout the ensuing period of Greek pre-eminence, horses were used mainly for draw-

Below *Rameses II chases the fleeing Nubians. The energy and determination of Rameses II led to the expansion of Egypt before the final decline of her extensive empire. The chariot by this time had spoked wheels and would be drawn by horses of the finest quality—probably purchased from wandering nomads. Egypt later became the main supplier of horses.*

ing chariots. The utmost care was devoted to breeding and great expense was incurred in the maintenance of studs. The great horse-keepers and winners of the chariot races were inevitably princes and ruling families: the cost of caring for horses put them beyond the means of all but the very rich.

The Greeks seem to have bred both light and heavy horses and used each for its specific purpose. But the more beautiful and swift a horse, the more likely it was to be a race horse, and that it belonged to a rich family. Although the use of cavalry was widespread throughout Greece in those early times, its use was very limited and much greater dependence rested on the use of infantry. The war-horse was undervalued and the race-horse venerated. It is interesting to note, in this context, that the finest users of horses in battle throughout history have been those races whose powers of establishing a sophisticated, cultural civilization have been least adequate.

Alexander the Great

In the fourth century BC, however, under the rules of Philip of Macedon and his son Alexander the Great, a more extensive and imaginative use of cavalry was made. King Philip, indeed, is credited with having originated the cavalry charge. Mounted soldiers had previously fought in scattered fashion, each performing his personal feats: Philip seems to have been the first military leader to order his horsemen to drill for a massed charge.

Bucephalus

It is related that Alexander won his famous stallion, Bucephalus, from his father. The boy Alexander would not be prevented from riding the beautiful animal, though, being of high fettle and skittish, with rolling eyes and flared nostrils, it had already defeated some of the best riders in Philip's army. Having noticed that the horse was probably frightened by its own shadow, Alexander took its bridle and turned its head towards the sun. Then the boy mounted and rode the calmed animal. The king was so impressed that he made Alexander a present of Bucephalus.

Bucephalus was nearly 30 years old when he was killed in the battle between Alexander and Porus, King of India. Mortally wounded, and

Left *The Assyrian chariot
was of a much heavier
build than those of its
predecessors, being able
to carry more soldiers and
requiring more horses to
pull it. So essential was the
chariot to their forms of
warfare and so vast were
the areas which they
travelled, that the Assy-
rians were forced to
provide for repairs on
their campaigns.*

Far left *The use of the
chariot in lands of the
Israelites was much
restricted by their terrain
and their difficulties in
procuring horses. Here a
reconstruction of an ivory
plaque from Megiddo,
Canaan, shows wooden
chariots with six-spoked
wheels and a central axle.*

surrounded by attackers, Bucephalus carried his master to safety against all odds. Alexander later named a city, Bucephalia, in his horse's honour.

From the age of 13, Alexander had been placed for four years under the care of Aristotle, by whom he was instructed in the art of politics and the art of war. Trained to be expert in all manly exercises, in the use of arms, and in horsemanship, he proved an able pupil. When only 18, in 338 BC, he fought at his father's side at the Battle of Chaeronea, where his extraordinary deployment of cavalry divisions and his courage resulted in victory.

The influence of Xenophon

There is no doubt that Alexander learned much of his skill in handling horses from Xenophon, a fourth century BC horseman and leader, whose writings on the horse are perhaps the most important to have survived from ancient Greece.

Xenophon was the man who, more than any other ancient, realized the effectiveness of the horse in war. In order to obtain the greatest

Opposite page above *Highly skilled Sythian horsemen decorate this sixth century BC bronze Greek bowl. Making feigned retreats then turning to fire at the pursuer was a favourite ploy of the Parthians who were to inflict devastating defeats upon Roman armies in later centuries.*

Opposite page bottom right *A Roman two-horse chariot from the first century AD.*

Opposite page bottom left *A centaur tramples down a Lapith. For a long time Greek superstition prevented them from riding—a man mounted on a horse being likened to a centaur.*

Above left *For a long time the conditions in Greece did not favour the use of the horse in war. By 550 BC, however, mounted warriors began to appear on the scene, although the infantry continued to predominate in the warfare of this period.*

Left *Many of the finest horses in Ancient Greece were kept solely for racing purposes. In this scene, taken from an amphora from Vulci, two youths race on rather over-sized horses.*

Above *A statuette thought to be of Alexander the Great, dating from the Roman Imperial period. It was Alexander who was the first to realise the effectiveness of a combination of cavalry and infantry, using the cavalry for its shock value after the enemy had been checked by the Macedonian phalanx.*

efficiency from horses in battle, he argued, they should be bred and trained carefully, and afterwards treated carefully. Kindness, he knew, achieved more than any other method. All the knowledge and skill he collected was written down, so that the collective knowledge of hundreds of years was gathered together and formulated into a code of practice.

His feet should be hollow and ring like cymbals. The pastern should be sloping but not too much so. The horse should have good bones, supple knees, powerful shoulders and a broad chest; the neck should not sag, but be arched like the neck of a fighting cock.

This arching gave greater protection to the rider, who could see better and direct the horse more effectively. The head had to be lean, the cheek small, and the eye prominent, nostrils wide, crest large, ears small, withers high, loins short and broad, shoulder high and haunches wide.

Xenophon, however, was in a minority. In general, the Hellenic culture was a culture of the mind, and as a nation of fighters they are to be measured by men such as Philip of Macedon and his son, Alexander the Great, represented charging at the head of his cavalry on the mosaic of the battle of Arbela, inspiring his army with his own ardour. The deeds of battle of these two men represent the highest achievement of the warlike spirit in Greece.

The Roman Empire

Because of the size of her dominions, it was necessary for Rome to maintain an army capable of crushing all signs of rebellion occurring in any of the distant regions. The Roman army was founded principally on the legion, the phalanx and engines of war; they used horses mainly for hauling, for chariots and for light skirmishing cavalry. Mercenaries were often used in light cavalry units; able, native horsemen were recruited from Syria, Arabia and North Africa. It was natural, such vast regions having been conquered, that horses of other countries should have been confiscated and used by the Roman armies. Particular favourites were the Arabian warm-blooded horses, which they used in cavalry wings.

Early in the Christian period, their war horses were mainly of Northern breeds: Friesians, Bergundians and Cappadocians for pulling their heavy chariots, Persians for saddle horses, and Spanish and North African breeds for stud and haulage. There was a definite love of quality in horse flesh at this time and so extreme were the lengths to which some Romans were prepared to go for their horses that incredible stories have come down to the present day about their horse worship. Celebrated individual horses were treated royally. Their hooves were painted with gilt, and they were given lavish presents. Caligula, the mad emperor, is said to have presented

Above *There was a definite love of horses of quality in Imperial Rome, especially among the highest members of the state and at times this was taken to extreme lengths. This Roman bronze of the first century BC shows an artist's imaginative concept of the wild and spirited Arab horse.*

Above *A bas-relief showing the Roman infantry and cavalry. Drawn mainly from the elite of society, the Roman cavalry often proved an ineffective element in early warfare.*

Right *The Greek historian and essayist, Xenophon, whose writings on the horse were to propound many accepted ideas of the twentieth century.*

Far right *Hannibal confronts Africanus across the river. In contrast to the Romans, Hannibal's army was always equipped with the finest possible mounts.*

a favourite horse, Incitatus, with a house and furniture, and to have insisted that friends came to dine with the horse; they were further expected to invite Incitatus to dine at their own homes!

Such indulgent treatment was not, however, the lot of most horses of the time. The Roman Empire was forged in war and it continued by means of war. In so bellicose an age, the horse was an essential element in communication, transport and fighting.

The aristocracy was the main power behind the cavalry wings used to supplement the Roman infantry. The general lack of effectiveness of the cavalry may be attributed to the fact that it was drawn from what was an effete element of Roman society. The cavalry was often merely a foraging element, used to mop up retreating enemies;

although when the Romans encountered fine horsemen, such as the Goths or the Britons, they were glad to depend on the cavalry and even eager to recruit local tribesmen. But it remained a continual complaint throughout Roman times that there was never enough money spent upon the cavalry, with the result that they tended always to be a potential weakness.

Hannibal—the master of the horse

One of the most exacting enemies ever to face the Romans was Hannibal. Towards the end of the third century BC Hannibal, tactician and leader of cavalry, disorganized and devastated the Roman armies. He is probably best known for his crossing of the Alps with his war elephants: that he was a master of horse is not so well known.

Top *The greatest dependence of most armies of this period was still placed in the well-armoured infantryman.*

Above *Hannibal recruited many allies in his hazardous trek through the Alps. Here a Gaul engages the Roman Servili Puley in combat.*

Hannibal's father taught him in boyhood to swear eternal enmity to Rome. It was a vow he was to keep.

The Numidians who formed Hannibal's cavalry arm in his forced march on Rome must have presented an awesome sight. Each rider sat upon a beautiful, superbly equipped horse of Arab stock; a horse with powerful chest and neck, superb wind and speed. The Roman horses, in contrast, were principally of the small, rough pony breeds. Only the generals could afford the well-bred Arabic horses. Moreover, there was always a lack of homogeneity about the Roman cavalry, owing to their extensive recruitment of mercenaries from the area in which the Romans happened to be fighting.

Having crossed the Alps in 15 days, Hannibal drew up his army, his elephants in the centre, his cavalry on the wings. Separating the two were lines of infantry; Hannibal was well aware that the smell of elephants drove horses mad. The Roman cavalry discovered this fact too late as they drew near and in the following clash, they suffered a major defeat.

The Parthians

In 53 BC, the Romans, led by Crassus, suffered a most humiliating defeat at the hands of a superior force of Parthian horsemen. The Romans had been following what they believed to be a small force of Parthians. Suddenly, that small force stopped, turned, and was joined from nearby woods by hordes of screaming horsemen with painted faces. As they bore down on the amazed

Romans, Crassus tried to organize his men but, still riding forward, the Parthians fired a withering rain of arrows upon the Roman phalanx. The Romans were several times drawn into following the Parthians as they appeared to retreat but they would turn half-round in their saddles and loose another stream of deadly arrows at their unfortunate pursuers.

Crassus' son, Publius, was leading the Roman cavalry, which consisted mainly of Gauls. Though they were agile, leaping from their horses to stab the Parthian horses in the belly, they suffered terrible casualties from the arrows, because they wore only light armour. Publius was killed and his head carried around on a spear. As the Roman cavalry collapsed, the Parthian horsemen were able further to harass the Roman infantry; eventually, Crassus, too, was slain and his head impaled. The battle of Carrhae was a black episode in the history of Rome.

The Britons

In 55 BC, Caesar invaded Britain. Aware of the quality of native horsemen in general, he assembled a force of about two legions (10,000 soldiers); of these, approximately 600 would have been cavalry. Having embarked safely, the all-important cavalry failed to arrive on the English coast at the same time as the infantry. Huge seas and storms had battered the ships and many of the horses were drowned.

On attempting to land, Caesar was to learn to his cost of the quality and skill of the Briton on horseback. The white cliffs swarmed with barbarous warriors, tattooed in blue woad, screaming their war cries and riding backwards and forwards on their tireless, tough little horses. Lightly armed, the Britons were able to flash in among the small pockets of stranded soldiery attempting to gain the shore, and to retreat to higher ground before the Romans could re-form. Eventually, the Romans managed to form up around their standards, in time to see the Britons disappear like phantoms into the nearby woodlands.

While the main force pitched camp, the Roman

Right *The Ancient Britons were renowned for their ferocity, often charging into battle with swords fixed to their chariot wheels.*

Below *Many though were the deficiencies of the Roman cavalry, they increased in importance as the barbarian attacks grew in frequency and effect. The armour of these 'barbarians' would be made from some soft material, probably leather. The advance of horse armour can also be seen although the coats would never have been as close-fitting as these.*

An Ancient Briton in a War Chariot in the Action of Attack with his Target, Spear &c.

7th Legion made a foraging expedition. As they gathered corn some distance from their base camp, they were attacked by a force of British horsemen. The novel and terrifying tactics of the natives threw the Romans into disorder. As well as attacking from all sides on their small and nimble horses, the Britons drove chariots, drawn by two horses, one on either side of a central shaft, with incredible skill out of the woodlands and straight at the scattered Romans. They were confused and terrified by war cries, the cracking of whips and the thunder of chariot wheels. Such was the Briton's skill that they could check their steeds in full gallop down a steep slope. They made lightning turns and dashes and the chariot driver was able to run out on the slender pole between his horses and deliver his spears with terrifying accuracy. When the chariots had been driven among the enemy, the drivers dismounted and fought like infantry before again leaping onto their frightening engines of war and galloping into the dark woods. Only the approach of Caesar himself saved the 7th Legion in this crisis.

The same deadly tactics with cavalry and chariots were used by the British queen Boadicea of Iceni, a tribe who lived in what is now East Anglia. The governor of Britain, Suetonius Paulinus, was fighting in Anglesey; his subordin-ate, Catus, had for some unknown reason ordered the scourging of the widowed Boadicea and the violation of her two daughters. The Iceni and their neighbouring tribe, the Trinobantes, rode down in fearful vengeance upon the Roman settlements at Colchester, London and St. Albans. A Roman legion of 500 men was massacred; Queen Boadicea, in a blood-red cloak, drove a chariot with knives embedded in the wheels, cutting her way through the Roman phalanx. Tacitus placed the number of Romans killed by her apocalyptic horsemen at over 70,000. It took the concentrated might of the returned general, Suetonius, to defeat this wild and most terrifying British queen; in AD 61, she ended her own life by swallowing poison.

Adrianople and the fall of Rome
Their failure to learn the lessons of their defeats and to build up and use their cavalry forces more effectively eventually cost the Romans dearly. Tribes of Goths and Huns, accustomed from childhood to fighting on horseback, began to invade the crumbling Roman Empire. The most significant blow of all came at the battle of Adrianople, in AD 378, when Gothic horsemen soundly defeated the infantry in which Rome had taken such great pride.

Below *The Germanic tribes posed a continual threat to the Romans and border clashes were savage and brutal—often leading to reprisal raids. It was at border regions such as this that the horse was the most essential element.*

The age of the horse

After the fourth century, with the gradual disappearance of the Roman occupiers, a period of great social upheaval began throughout Britain and Europe. Itinerant and often war-like tribes came and went; some settled, others wandered further. The prime element of a successful warring tribe was the horse; when conditions deteriorated, it could carry its rider quickly and efficiently to the next temporary site.

Attila—the Scourge of God

At the time of the fall of the Roman Empire, the acknowledged world master of military horse strategy was Attila the Hun. Known to his enemies as the Scourge of God, Attila's proud boast was that wherever his horse had stepped, the grass would never grow again. Attila and his brother, Bleda, succeeded to the throne in AD 434. They ruled over almost all the tribes north of the Danube, and their kingdom stretched from the frontiers of Gaul to the borders of China.

It is unthinkable that Attila would have been the terror of the known world without his command of and use of horses. He almost lived in the saddle. Indeed, on one of the first occasions that the ambassadors of Constantinople were suing for peace with Attila, he refused to dismount from his superb Tartary-bred warhorse, imposing the arrogance of his mounted position upon the ignominy of their standing. When returning from his victories, Attila would have one of his innumerable wives lay a silver table with choice delicacies. The table would then be lifted, so that Attila could eat while remaining in the saddle.

In one of his final battles, at Chalons sur Marne, Attila employed his favourite technique of descending upon the enemy in three wings, employing up to 300,000 horsemen, all of them equipped with the fiery and tough steeds bred from the Tartary strains of cold-blooded Equus Caballus. These three wings, with Attila himself at the centre, would sweep down upon their enemies, with the left and right mounted sections swinging in a crescent-shaped arc to pierce the flanks and rear of the opposition. The effect of these tactics on all armies, including those of the Romans, was devastating and the Huns roamed at will across the wastes of eastern Europe, pillaging and burning. Finally, however, at Chalons sur Marne, the leader of the Visigoths, a chieftain named Torismond, proved a match for Attila, who was forced back into a small village where he took shelter for the night. Within a fortified circle of wagons, Attila ordered a huge pile of saddles

Checa's fiery and imaginative interpretation of Atilla and the Huns during the sack of Rome. Until Atilla came to the fore as leader, the Huns had often fought with other tribes and had taken part in the battle of Adrianople where their allies and enemies had learnt of their amazing ability to ride swiftly and determinedly and fire arrows accurately at the same time. However, their incredible mobility was put to a mainly destructive use.

and horse furniture, including horse furs and draperies, to be gathered together into a huge pyre, so that if the enemy did manage to break through, then he, Attila, could die in the fire from his beloved horse belongings. Unfortunately, Torismond did not follow up his attack and Attila and his cavalry were able to make their escape.

When Attila died, in AD 453, his body was solemnly laid out in the middle of a plain under a silken pavilion. For days, the great squadrons of horsemen he had led so magnificently wheeled and rode around the imposing catafalque, playing the martial music that had always accompanied their charges and chanting funeral songs to the great and magical king who with his savage hordes had broken the last remnants of the Roman Empire. The terror of the world was dead and his remains enclosed within three coffins, one of silver, one of gold and one of iron, drawn by a team of the finest horses in the kingdom and buried privately in the night with all his richest spoils.

Cavalry techniques

As the centuries went by, various developments, such as the invention of the stirrup in the eighth century, laid the basis for the finer evolution of cavalry techniques in later ages. The Roman phalanx or the infantry of Macedonia had never had to face such firmly seated horsemen as were to come later. In those primitive centuries, however, about which so little is known and to which we now refer as the Dark Ages, some of the basic and abiding systems of cavalry technique were

Above *During the Dark Ages the stirrup came into use in the West. In Ancient China, however, it had probably been in use since the fourth century. Without this essential element of equipment the heavy cavalryman would never have been able to retain his seat against the shock of a lance's impact.*

Right *The lineal predecessors of the Mongols, the Huns blazed a trail of fear and destruction through Europe. The ugliness of man and horse played a valuable role in psychological warfare.*

evolved, by men who were not military strategists in any technical sense, but simply men who lived with horses. They knew exactly what their horses could do and how those capabilities could be used to advantage in battle conditions.

It seems that there were two essential developments in the progress of the military horse after the eighth century AD. In Europe, generally speaking, the soldier who rode upon horseback grew heavier and heavier as his personal armour increased in size and weight; with the introduction of horse armour, the burden borne by each individual beast was enormous. The development of heavier, stronger horses was essential to take the weight of the heavy panoply of mail; consequently, the native beauty, grace and elegance of the horse were sacrificed to the qualities of power and endurance. King John was one who contributed to the improvement of the breed of heavy horses for agricultural and war use. He imported into Britain over 100 Flanders stallions, which probably laid the foundation of the strength and size characteristic of our horses of war and labour.

The second development took place essentially in the Middle East and Asia Minor, where lighter, more agile and swifter horses were being bred to serve the needs of the Ottoman Sultans, the Chinese Emperors, the Tartar War Lords and the Mongolian Princes. And it was in those distant places, with the magic names of Samarkand, Persepolis, Acre and Constantinople, that the finest and most imaginative uses of the horse in war were to be found. This is not to say that the lighter horsemen in Europe, a progressively developing arm of the fighting kings, did not

have their place but they were used very little. It was not really until West met East, in those desultory and migratory encounters known as the Crusades, that the superiority of the lightly armed, swiftly mounted horsemen was established over the ponderous and anonymous knight, encased in iron, who took an age to gain an impetus that could be squandered in a moment if the enemy refused to remain static.

These developments, of course, took place over hundreds of years, but, until the progressive and deadly development of guns and cannon, the horse remained a supremely imaginative and decisive element in the battle and war strategies of the first generals. William the Conqueror, for example, owed his victory in the Battle of Hastings to his cavalry and he paid very close attention to the development of English breeds of horse.

After the Battle of Hastings, the manner of using cavalry seems to have differed in England from that in, for example, the wilder areas of Scotland, Wales and Ireland. The English, probably much influenced by Norman example, seemed to prefer heavy armour and large, strong horses, as we might infer from this account of London sports, written before 1183 by William Fitzstephen, secretary to Thomas à Becket:

'In the suburbs immediately outside one of the

Above *Horses often played an essential part in the religions of the period. The chief of the Norse gods and the god of war, Odin, was thought to have ridden about the world on an eight-legged horse called Sleipner. Above fly the ravens Hugin (*thought*) and Munnin (*memory*) as his news gatherers.*

Left *A section from the colourful Norwegian Baldishon Tapestry showing early armour. For a long time the knights would have been dressed in chain mail with no solid metal trappings.*

Above *Three scenes from the Bayeux tapestry.*
Left *Disembarking the Norman horses after their precarious voyage across the Channel.* **Centre** *The Norman advance. Whilst the English held their shields in formation they were relatively safe. However,* **Right,** *a feigned retreat by the Normans drew the English out of their defensive group and led to defeat. It is interesting to note that the spears are not yet being held in the traditional manner for a lance but are still being held over-arm.*

Right *By the twelfth century armour was well developed for both horse and rider. The horse's head, neck and chest are all well-protected and the rider is almost fully encased in chain-mail. The saddle is becoming more like the armchair design which made it much more difficult for the knight to be unseated in battle.*

gates there is a smooth field, both in fact and in name (Smithfield). On every sixth day of the week, unless it be a major feast day on which solemn rites are prescribed, there is a much frequented show of fine horses for sale. Thither come all the Earls, Barons and Knights who are in the city and with them many of the citizens, whether to look on or buy. It is a joy to see . . . the costly destriers of graceful form and goodly stature with quivering ears, high necks and plump buttocks. . . . When a race between such trampling steeds is about to begin . . . their limbs tremble, impatient of delay, they cannot stand still. When the signal is given, they stretch forth their limbs they gallop away, they rush on with obstinate speed.'

The whole passage is suffused with an instinct about and a knowledge of horses. The same writer confirms in the following passage how all young men are ready and eager for fighting, irrespective of the age in which they live. The war horse of the Middle Ages was in a very real sense an extension of the ferocity, the arrogance and the spirit of the men of those times:

'Every Sunday in Lent, after dinner, a fresh swarm of young gentles goes forth on war horses . . . from the households of Earls and Barons come young men not yet invested with the belt of Knighthood, that they may there contend to-

gether. Each one of them is on fire with the hope of victory. The fierce horses neigh, their limbs tremble; they champ the bit, impatient of delay they cannot stand still. When at length the hoof of trampling steeds careers along, the youthful riders divide their hosts; some pursue those that fly before and cannot overtake them, others unhorse their comrades and speed by.'

This aspect of preparedness for war seems to have been picked out by contemporary writers. When Richard I's fleet left for the third Crusade, one of the ships was said to be laden with forty horses 'of price'; all of them well trained for war and with all kinds of arms for as many riders. The ship also contained a year's food for both the men and the horses and this highlights one of the greatest weaknesses of the medieval cavalry units who depended upon the closed charge: the question of food. Much of it was carried in wagons and apportioned daily, whereas the horses of tribesmen living, for example, in Wales and Scotland were tougher and better able to subsist on the sparse grassland of their mountainous homes.

Native pony breeds

It was not only the toughness of small pony breeds that enabled them to fare well in war, but also their agility. Robert the Bruce employed

Above *The anonymity of medieval armour eventually lead to the devising of heraldry as a means of identifying the enemy. Each knight would either carry his own device or that of his overlord.*

techniques of hit and fly in his battle with the English in 1314 at Bannockburn. With a force only one third of the strength of the English King, Edward II, he defeated the heavy and ponderous English knights. When the great horses of England charged the pikes of the Scots, it was as if they had smashed into a thick forest. There was a great and terrible clashing of spears and the sharp snapping of oak staffs and of destriers wounded to the death. Huge knights were unseated and stranded on their backs like bright beetles, while the nimble Scots leapt off their ponies to kill the helpless riders. Many of the heavy English horses and their riders fell into the ditches of that rough terrain, horse upon horse, knight upon knight, a plunging, heaving confusion of fallen fighting men, helpless and at the mercy of their swift and deadly adversaries.

It was the Scottish army's power that they were, almost to a man, on horseback. Their knights and squires were always well-horsed; the common people and others rode on little hacks and geldings. They took with them no carts or chariots because of the mountainous terrain. Nor did they carry bread or wine, being very abstemious when at war. They would travel great distances and endure any hardship, drinking only river water, carrying no pots and pans, preferring to cook any animal caught in its skin. They carried everything they needed on their horses. Between the saddle and the pannell, they carried a metal plate and behind the saddle, a little sack of oatmeal. When occasion presented, they cooked small cakes on the metal plate heated over a fire. These marauding armies of Scots horsemen, by the very nature of their mobility, could cover enormous distances with little cost.

The Welsh warriors of the late twelfth century had the same spartan qualities as their forebears in the time of the Roman Occupation. They made use of light arms, which did not impede their agility; small coats of mail, bundles of arrows and

Below *The Scots had long been using horses. This Pictish slab from Invergowrie, Angus, shows a ninth-century horseman.*

Below right *Although the native Scots would be mounted on small ponies, the Scottish nobility would be indistinguishable from the Anglo-Normans.*

long lances, helmets and shields and, more rarely, greaves plated with iron. The higher classes went into battle mounted upon swift and generous Welsh-bred horses. The horsemen, whenever the situation or occasion provided, were quite content to fight as infantry, whether attacking or retreating. In order to keep themselves fit, in time of peace, they penetrated the deepest forests and climbed the most difficult mountains, learning by practice to endure fatigue through day and night; and as they meditated on war during peacetimes, they would extend their meditations by daily practice in the use of the lance and hardening their bodies for the difficulties of war. Like the Scottish fighters, they were not addicted to gluttony or drunkenness. They incurred no expense in food or clothes and their thoughts were bent solely on self-protection. To this end, they continuously employed themselves in the care of their horses and their tackle. They fasted from morning until evening; they were not deterred by the cold, the dark or hunger. They thought single-mindedly of their enemies and how they might be outwitted.

However effective the native Celtic elements might be in their treatment of and fighting use of the horse, and though the future would show their native instincts and abilities in the management of horses to be the finer, the times lay with the heavy horse and the dull and generally unimaginative initial charge, by which one attempted to grind one's enemy into the dust. The principal set-piece battle in Europe, between the Norman Conquest and the time of Henry VIII, had this technique as its main attacking element. It was a system that, set against the ghost-like cavalry exploits of the Ottoman Turks, was shown to be primitive to the point of absurdity.

The growth of chivalry

The development of the heavy horse and knights in battle really had its roots in the ideas of nobility,

Below *The trappings of knighthood. Being girded with sword, armour, belt and spurs.*

Bottom *An illumination from the French Arthurian legends showing the knights engaged in savage combat.*

Below *The height of the medieval ideal of chivalry as personified in the gallant knight, St George, who with love-given bravery, slew the fire-breathing dragon to save the imperilled maiden.*

Below right *The pageantry of medieval life—a spring procession taken from the Book of Hours.*

Far right above *Delacroix's romantic conception of the Crusader's Entry into Constantinople.*

Far right below *The tournament originally a valuable training ground for war, increasingly devolved into a ceremonial occasion—the board being set up to prevent serious injury.*

or comitatus, which originated principally among the tribes of north-west Gaul. The idea was very simple. If a battle occurred between warring tribes, then it was decreed that no-one should leave the battlefield until the Lord or Chieftain did so. It was further decreed that, if the chieftain should die in battle, every member of his tribe who was fighting on the battlefield had to give up his life fighting also. It was a very severe principle, involving a highly developed sense of duty and justice with very little regard for the self.

These ideas took root later, especially among the Anglo-Saxons, whose poetry records the many battles fought; such as at Maldon, in which, the lord having been slain, his retinue would then fight to the bitter end. Gradually, out of this idea grew the principle of chivalry and the growing influence of Christianity ensured that the two separate ideas, one pagan and one Christian, grew together to form one noble and all-embracing ethic. The ideal of chivalry formed one of the brightest threads in the rich tapestry of medieval life.

Lessons of the Crusades

The ideas that lay behind the social behaviour of medieval people had their finest expression in the Crusades, where the principle of Christian ethic was set against the 'pagan' ideology. Until the end of the eleventh century, the milites were the warriors who, protected by mail shirt, steel cap and shield, fought on horseback with sword and lance. In the late eleventh century and in the twelfth century, there were two important developments. First, knighthood became a social distinction, synonymous with nobility and aristocracy; the milites became a caste, initiated by ceremony. Secondly, defensive armour became much more elaborate; by the end of the twelfth century, the horse and the armour had become much heavier, and what is more important, more expensive. Alongside this development, there was the growing need for a lightly armed and more agile horseman, and this need was, to a limited extent, met by the class of horseman known as Sergants à Cheval.

These groups of horsemen were sent on speculative missions to reconnoitre and often to skirmish with the enemy. Often, too, the Sergants à Cheval were put in charge of spare horses that would be used by the Knights at Arms. The first attack would be made by the heavy knights, holding the lance in their right hand and the reins and shield in their left. Such attacks always depended

upon surprise, upon massed weight and, most important of all, the willingness of the enemy to remain fixed while the charge was made. The power of such charges was obvious and it was said that a Frank on horseback would make a hole through the walls of Babylon.

Such primitive uses of horses in battle were soon to be found wanting, when those costly, heavy horses were set against the light marauding bands of the Saracen hordes. The indications of the quality of the Turkish horsemen were seen,

for example, in their fighting with the Franks. The Turks would never wait to be charged; they were never still, forming and reforming their ranks in bewildering fashion. The most effective part of the Turkish army was always on horseback. They were quicker and more effective than the Franks, their horses were lighter, of greater pace and agility, and the lightness of their weapons added to their speed. As well as a bow, they carried a shield, a lance, a sword and a club.

The Turkish riders always remained at a dis-

tance, like pale phantoms haunting the horizons. They were like a swarm of flies when engaged in the fight. They would employ the feigned retreat, such as had been practised in feudal Europe, and which had decided the Battle of Hastings. Sometimes, these false retreats would go on for days, wearying and confusing the enemy. Sometimes, a small and apparently vulnerable group of horsemen would be the bait for a sustained ambush; but principally the Turks would harass the flanks and rear of armies, especially when they were on the march.

Not only were these superb horsemen able to attack and disappear with the co-ordination of a flock of birds; they were also deadly users of bows and arrows, using them while riding at full speed in the saddle. Even in retreat, they would turn half round in their saddles and loose off a devastating rain of arrows. Their rate of fire was incredible and, in documents of the period, one of the recurring images of those who had suffered such an attack was to liken victims to porcupines, such was the number of arrows used. The second Crusade of 1147 and the warrior Frederick Barbarossa, in 1190, both suffered these tactics. Furthermore, the Turks were well aware that the most vulnerable point of enemy cavalry was the horse itself. They shot deliberately for the horse's vitals and thus broke the cohesion of the opposing battle plan. Eyewitnesses of the Crusades record the grave weakness caused to immigrant armies by the loss of large numbers of their horses, especially when crossing Asia Minor in the twelfth century. The Crusaders were often forced to use their horses as food when they found themselves in hostile terrain and this added further to their difficulties.

As ever in warfare, the exploitation of one system that proves successful is countered by a move from those who learn from their suffering. The Crusaders learned to make close formation, with very strict laws and punishments for anyone who broke ranks. In 1191, when King Richard began his southward march to Acre, he was attacked, as if by a swarm of bees, by Saladin's horsemen. Richard's army, however, maintained such a close formation that an eyewitness commented that it was not possible to toss a plum or an apple into the host without hitting a man or a horse.

Richard faced a similar problem on the day of the Battle of Arsuf. The Knights of St. John, in the rear of the army, were stung into retaliation by a band of Turks, who were riding close in and killing their horses; consequently, the knights broke ranks before the king had given the order. Later, the Knights Templars formulated very strict rules. The leaving of rank was strictly forbidden. A knight could only leave the rank to test his horse in a short gallop, or to rescue a Christian in imminent danger of death from a Muslim. Knights were to suffer severe punishments if they disobeyed the rule; one was the loss of habit and therefore the honour of fighting for

Christendom.

To show the extent of exhortation necessary to inspire troops facing Turkish horsemen, one might quote the case of Prince Roger of Antioch, who compelled his troops to resist Turkish provocation by mounting a fast horse and riding through the camp with a drawn sword, threatening death to any man who broke the rule. Not only did these tactics help to cut down losses, but by their success they turned the Christian commanders' ideas towards other methods of fighting, one of which was to have horsemen and infantry working very closely together; this technique worked so well that the Turks found themselves spending a great deal of energy on separating horse and foot soldiers. Such was the success of these new forms of resistance to Turkish cavalry attacks that, by the time of King Richard's attack at Jaffa, in 1192, the Turks had actually been discouraged even from making horse attacks in any great numbers.

The military mastodon

Despite what had been learned on the Crusades about mounting cavalry attacks, in Europe, the heavily armoured knight on a heavy horse continued to lead the field. Perhaps one of the finest exponents of the massed charge and subsequent hand-to-hand fighting between mounted knights was the Black Prince, who first fought at his father's side at the Battle of Crécy, in 1346, when he was only 17 years old. In the first of the battle positions was placed the young Prince of Wales, with the Earl of Warwick and other noblemen. There were 800 men at arms, 2000 archers and 1000 other soldiers. Each knight and lord drew to that part of the field appointed to him under his own heraldic banner and pennon.

The French knights, dressed in elaborate armour and part of an army of 60,000 men, made the first sortie against the well-positioned English. Then the English bowmen stepped forward one pace and loosed their arrows simultaneously. The sky darkened as if it had snowed, so thickly did their goose-tipped arrows fall. When the horses and knights suffered this swingeing flight, there was panic as horse fell upon horse and knights crashed to the ground. No horse could be spurred forward and there was no way back because of the confusion. The archers shot again into the place where the press was thickest and many Genoese crossbowmen in the French army cut their bowstrings and fled from the field, whereupon many of them were cut down by the furious French king.

At one point in time, riders came to the English king, saying his son, the Black Prince, was in great danger of being overwhelmed. And the King said: 'Is my son dead or on the earth felled?' 'No, Sir', said a knight, 'but he is in great danger and needs assistance from you'. 'Well,' said the King, 'return to him and to those that sent you hither, and say to them that they send no more to me for any adventure that falleth, as long as my

Opposite page
The romantic conception of the crusades by no means matched the reality. Both sides were, at least superficially, fighting for an ideal and the encounters were savage and at times inhuman—many horses bearing the impact of the battle.

Overleaf *It was at Agincourt that the effectiveness of the long-bow against the massed charge of heavy horsemen was demonstrated —the English winning against amazingly overwhelming odds.*

son is alive: and also say to them, that they suffer him this day to win his spurs; for if God be pleased, I will this journey be his, and the honour thereof, and to them that be about him'. Eventually, the Prince was able to fight his way out of the main battle and, by skilful deployment of his cavalry against the enemy flank, managed to turn the tide of battle in favour of the English. He had certainly lived up to the iron expectation his father had of both his courage and his ability.

In 1356, the Prince again revealed how fine a general he was. Using his cavalry to tempt the French into an ambush, he deployed one of the characteristics so beloved of the Turks. The French heavy cavalry were vanquished, their horses shot from under them by mounted English bowmen, and their toppled knights slain in hundreds by English fighters, running among the fallen knights, carrying great knives and committing dreadful slaughter.

By the time of Agincourt, in October 1415, the size and weight of French horse and armour had become grotesque. King Henry V had occupied a very narrow and advantageous position, which allowed him to deploy small groups of light horsemen, many of them carrying bows, around his main defensive position. The French had been on horseback all night, and it had rained; the pages and grooms leading the horses about had cut up the soft ground so that the horses could scarcely raise their hooves. The French were so loaded with armour that they could not support themselves effectively or move forward with any degree of accuracy. They were armed with very heavy coats of steel, reaching to the knees or lower over the leg harness; and besides plate armour many of them had hooded helmets. This colossal weight of armour, together with the softness of the ground, made them almost immovable, so that the raising of clubs proved almost

impossible. They were faced with overwhelming problems, not the least of which was their inability to see through the many banners around them. Like the great mammals that ruled the world before their huge development rendered their extinction inevitable, the French knights of Agincourt heralded the end of a military mastodon.

Genghis Khan

While the knight and his charger ruled the battlefields of Europe in the late Middle Ages, the great vastnesses of Asia Minor gave birth to two of the most devastating leaders of horse the world has ever known: the legendary figures of Genghis Khan and Tamurlaine the Great.

The name of Genghis Khan is a name that over centuries has inspired dread and terror: the scourge of the world, this violent Tartar whose hordes conquered much of the known world; the Perfect Warrior, who in his time was reputed to have caused the deaths of over 5,000,000 human beings; the nomad chieftain who emerged from the region of the Gobi desert waged war upon the civilized nations of the world and defeated them. It is incredible that this herder of beasts outgeneralled the concentrated powers of three empires; that by his ability to organize, control and manage armies of horsemen, this barbarian humbled armies three times as large as his own and compelled comparison centuries later with such all-time military geniuses as Julius Caesar and Napoleon.

Born in 1164, the son of a Mongol chief, Genghis' early years were spent in considerable hardship, always on the move and being trained from an early age in all martial arts. His original name was Temujin, which means 'the finest steel'. He exchanged this name for Genghis Khan, which means 'the Khan of all the Khans', when

Below Poitiers, *the height of the Black Prince's career, revealed his masterly generalship. Using his cavalry to decoy the French, in the manner of the Turks, his archers unleashed their arrows into their midst and won a resounding victory.*

Below right The military mastodon. Weighed down increasingly with armour, the days of the heavy horse on the field of battle were fast becoming numbered.*

Opposite The battle of Rosebeck demonstrated the paradox of the gun, growing in use since the midfourteenth century, and the armoured knight, whose armour was becoming increasingly redundant.*

Bataille de Rosebecque.

Top *Genghis Khan, leader and unifier of the Mongol tribes.*

Centre *Unlike the pacifist Chinese, who were over-run by the Mongols, the Japanese were an essentially warlike nation. This screen shows a Japanese general at the battle of Uji river.*

Right *Joshua and his men in medieval armour.*

he became supreme ruler over the Mongols and Tartars. His father died when Genghis was only 14 and he was quickly forced into managing men and organizing them into fighting groups. In 1202, he defeated his own father-in-law, the Khan of the Keraites, and annexed his dominions. Gradually, he united under his personality all the fiery nomadic tribes of central Asia and in 1206 he was proclaimed Khan of all the Kingdoms. After gathering a vast army together, he invaded China in 1210. The Chinese Emperor made peace and married his daughter to Genghis, but, three years later, Peking and the northern provinces had been added to the Mongol empire. In 1218, Genghis Khan, with an army of 700,000 men, defeated Mohammed Kothbeddin, the greatest ruler of southern Asia. Eventually, Genghis Khan's empire stretched from the Volga to the Pacific and from Siberia to the Persian Gulf.

In battle, fighting under his personal standard of nine white yak tails, Genghis was inevitably supreme. First, he would send innumerable spies among the enemy to gain information, which would be carried back to the main army by fast horsemen; Napoleon employed this tactic with equal success some 600 years later. Next went the advance points, some 200 riders, scattered over the countryside in pairs; behind these scouts at a distance came the advance cavalry, some 30,000 picked warriors on the finest horses, each leading a spare horse. In close touch with the advance guard came the main hordes, led by the Khan himself. They came in hundreds of thousands, the dust raised by the thunder of their hooves blotting out the sun. Genghis Khan always led the centre, placing himself, actually and symbolically, at the front of his troops. Genghis had, as Napoleon was later to have, a personal Imperial Guard: 1000 of the finest Mongol veterans in his army, each one mounted upon a black horse and protected by leather armour which was polished till it shone like silver. One day, in his red silken pavilion at Karakorum, he asked one of the officers of his Imperial Guard what in all the world would bring the greatest happiness. 'The open steppe, a clear day and swift horse under you', replied the officer, 'and a falcon on your wrist to start up hares'. 'No', replied the Khan. 'To crush your enemies, to see them fall at your feet, to take their horses and goods and hear the lamentations of their women. That is the best'.

Underlying every campaign was the master organization of the veteran and successful leader and Genghis Khan knew that it was only by a scrupulous attention to detail that his success would last. At the centre of all his thinking was the horse; the pivotal element of his life and his success.

Even at the age of 56, he maintained the order, the discipline and the charisma that had made the legend. He would review his troops before battle, his knees drawn up high in the short stirrups, sitting in his high-peaked silver escutcheoned saddle set upon a milk-white stallion. In his high-brimmed white felt hat were eagle feathers, and red cloth streamers hung down in front of each ear like horns. His high long-sleeved black sable coat was bound with a girdle of gold plates or cloth of gold, and he would ride silently between the drawn-up squadrons of his fighting men. The shock divisions had their horses encased in lacquered leather armour, some black and some red. Every man carried two bows and two quivers full of arrows, their feathers covered to protect them against dampness. Their helmets were light and serviceable, with an iron-studded leather thong to protect the neck behind. Only those members of the army who were in the Khan's Imperial Guard carried shields. Besides a sabre, the men of the heavy cavalry had an axe hanging from their belts and a length of rope—lariats or cords for pulling siege engines and bogged-down carts. The amount they carried was minimal: leather sacks holding nosebags for the ponies and pots for the men, wax and files for sharpening the arrow heads, and spare bow strings. Each man carried emergency rations—smoke-cured meat and dry milk curds. The dried milk could be heated in water. In bad weather in mountainous districts, the hooves of the unshod ponies were bound up in strips of yak skin to protect them. When the men were desperate for food they would sometimes open one of the horse's veins in order to drink a small quantity of blood before closing the vein again.

When such hardships were suffered, Genghis Khan would become particularly mean. He was once delayed at the town of Gtrar, by a governor named Inaljuk, for five months. Eventually, the man was captured alive and as punishment, the Khan ordered that molten silver should be poured into his ears and eyes and the town reduced to ashes.

In the great war with Mohammed Kothbeddin, the cavalry of Genghis Khan employed the manoeuvres of silence. The Mongol cavalry remained invisible until the hour of battle, and then they performed all the complicated procedures of the attack in total silence. During the day they obeyed only the signals given by moving the standards—signals that were repeated to the warrior horsemen of each squadron by the arm movements of an officer. At night, signals were given by the raising and lowering of coloured lanterns near the standard of the corps commander.

But Genghis Khan was not only a destroyer: he was an administrator of the first order. He formulated a complicated code of laws named the Yassa, which laid down disciplined methods for the development of social cohesion; laws that were so effective that some of them are still to be traced in the same region today. He also set up and organized the Yam or Mongol horse post, which was the fastest method of communication anywhere in the world in the thirteenth century.

Two generations after Genghis Khan, Marco

Above *The Cossacks, master horsemen, first appeared in the fifteenth century as bands of wild mercenaries. This fierce rider comes from the Don river area.*

Polo described in detail the extraordinary system of horse communication:

'Now you must know that the messengers of the Emperor travelling from Kambulu find at every twenty-five miles of the journey a station which they call the Horse Post House. And at each of these stations there is a large and handsome building for them to put up at. . . . At some of the stations there shall be four hundred horses, at others, two hundred. Even when the messengers have to pass through a roadless track where no hostel stands, still the stations are to be found. . . . In this way, the Emperor receives despatches from places ten day's journey off in one day and night. . . .

'Moreover there are men in these stations who, when there is a call for great haste, travel a good two hundred and fifty miles in the day and as much in the night. Everyone of these messengers wears a great wide belt set all over with bells, so that their bells are heard jingling a long way off. . . . And the speed at which they go is marvellous'.

Throughout his life, the horse was probably more dear to the heart of Genghis Khan than were people. He mastered the art of cavalry fighting and of fighting on the run, and in any kind of climate or terrain. The story is told of how the town of Liao-Yang was besieged without success by the Mongol hordes. So they abandoned their baggage, carts and supplies, in full sight of the townspeople, the Cathayans, and drew off with their horse herds as if giving up the struggle or fearing the approach of a relieving army. For two days, the Mongols rode away slowly, then shifted to their best horses and galloped back swiftly in a single night. They arrived back at the city at daylight just in time to find the Cathayans, who were convinced that the Mongols had fled, occupied in plundering the baggage trains and carrying the spoils inside their city walls, the gates of which were open. The unexpected return of the horsemen took them by surprise and the whole town was massacred.

Genghis Khan died in the Sung area of China in 1227. To prevent his enemies from discovering the loss to the Mongol nation, the warriors escorting the death car killed everyone they met on the long journey back to the Gobi. There, he was buried in a secret grave, whose site has long been lost. There is a bright legend among the Mongols that every year a ghostly white horse rides over the desert of the Gobi to the forest where the Khan was buried and there all night stands beside the grave.

Tamurlaine the Great

More than 100 years after the death of Genghis Khan came Tamurlaine the Great, his Persian name, Timur-i-lane, meaning Timur the lame. The great chieftain of central Asia, Tamurlaine set out, as did Napoleon after him, to establish a world empire. Both men used cavalry with extraordinary success to collect information from which strategy was planned; to destroy the enemy and then to follow up with relentless pursuits. Both men maintained a veteran guard who were always kept in reserve, to be used when danger was greatest; and both established complex systems and networks of spies before beginning any

Centre *Tamurlaine by Jean Leon Gérome. Tamurlaine's lust for bloodshed and conquest carried him over an area ranging from Turkey to India that would be extensive for a modern traveller.*

Left *The Mongol warrior was completely dependent on his horse and no part of their horde would be made up of infantry.*

campaign.

Tamurlaine believed that the secret of a fine horse lay in its breeding and he lavished large amounts of money to ensure that he received the finest examples of Arab horses trained for speed, endurance and courage.

His first large campaign was against Toktamish, a descendant of the legendary Genghis Khan. Tamurlaine assembled 100,000 cavalrymen, each with two horses and armed with bow, lance and a razor-sharp scimitar. This huge force of horsemen covered 1800 miles in 18 weeks. The quality and beauty of Tamurlaine's horses can be seen in the marvellous Chinese models of horses of the period, their essential characteristics being noble bearing and high spirit. This great force of men moved forward on a 30-mile-wide front and lived mainly off the land. When game meat was needed, the centre halted and the wings continued forward until a circle with a diameter of 10 miles was encompassed. All squadrons of riders then rode towards the middle until all the game encircled was trapped and killed.

When he had learned from his spies where

Toktamish was, Tamurlaine made camp, ate well and then charged the enemy under a cloud of arrows fired from the saddle. The wings of his charge curved like a giant crescent to pierce the flanks of the enemy and to scatter them into pockets to be killed with swords. Any groups left together were attacked by the veteran guard and finally the remnants of the scattered army were pursued relentlessly and Toktamish was taken prisoner. Tamurlaine continued as far as the Don, and even Russia was threatened, but he decided to return to Samarkand.

In 1388, Tamurlaine turned his attention south. After conquering as far as Delhi and Persia, he moved west against the Syrians, who were assisted by the Egyptians. Such was the speed of Tamurlaine's cavalry onslaughts that he took Damascus and drove the Egyptians as far as Acre; then he made camp at Aleppo and threatened the Turkish Empire, whose King Bayozid was away attacking Constantinople. Hearing of the threat from Tamurlaine, Bayozid returned with an army of 200,000 men. But he was searching for a phantom. The enemy army could not be found, wherever he searched. When it was too late, he found the cunning Tamurlaine behind him; Tamurlaine had seized Ankara and all the Turkish baggage train and supplies.

This great cavalry action proved the model for European nations of later centuries. The Turks were weary from forced marches and hunger, and the attack, when it came in the crescent groups under a swarm of arrows, proved decisive. Eventually, Bayozid was left with only his personal guard to surround and protect him. They were cut down without mercy, Bayozid was taken prisoner and the rags of his army pursued for distances up to 200 miles. It is a measure of Tamurlaine's greatness as a leader that he treated Bayozid as an honoured guest.

In 1402, Tamurlaine returned to Samarkand, honoured in Asia and in Europe, his greatness as a general being recognized and praised by such monarchs as Henry IV of England, Charles VII of France and Henry III of France.

The period of transition

By the Renaissance period, we know from the magnificent contemporary paintings and sculptures that the horse was symbolic of power, majesty, grace and beauty. The tournament was by now an important social occasion of the court; monarch and lord felt himself judged by the quality, the beauty and the number of his horses.

The demand for better breeding

That very practical English monarch Henry VII, aware of the importance of conserving breeding stock and of adding to his own stables, had passed an act to prohibit the export of horses from the kingdom. His son, Henry VIII, was to spend a great deal of money on buying horses for tournament and military use. It was to be expected that a man with the natural gifts of the young Henry should turn his attention to horsemanship, a potential field of distinction in almost all European countries of the period.

In 1520, Henry VIII met Francis I of France at what has come to be known in history as The Field of the Cloth of Gold. Henry was a man who had to shine in any company; his love of horses ensured that he would, as far as was possible, possess only the best. Unfortunately, comparison with the stables of European monarchs showed that the stables of England did not contain the best horses in the known world. The English had preserved the heavier horse that had distinguished itself in famous battles and on the tournament lists: strong and muscular, rather than fleet and spirited. Despite the strength of such animals, however, the Venetian ambassador Giustinian reported that King Henry VIII could tire at least eight strong horses in one hunting session.

It must have vexed Henry, at the Field of the Cloth of Gold, to find that his own horses were inferior to those of Francis. Henry's ambassadors had scoured Europe for fine-quality horses, especially breeding mares, usually from Flanders. At their meeting, both Francis and Henry preferred the excellent strain of horses being bred in Italy at that time where the famous stables at Mantua and Naples were producing horses that combined the best of European and Arabic strains. The quality of Arab blood was fast being recognized of paramount importance in breeding the animals most suitable for tournament and military use. When Henry's searchers found a particularly good horse, they were prepared to pay almost any price for it. Certainly, a horse was considered by most lords to be worth far more than one of their retainers.

Resistance to improvement

Although Henry had legislated for the breeding of bigger horses on all the large estates in England, the native English horse was not, as visiting ambassadors observed, a wonderful species. As in previous times, the best horses were to be found in Wales or in the stables of the aristocracy.

Some 50 years later, in Elizabeth's time, the raising of an army of suitably large horses for purposes of war was found to be very difficult. At first, special commissioners were appointed to make sure that each landowner, small or large, provided his fair share. But the counties responded badly and in 1569 the government was forced to tighten the rules; after this date, the responsibility for raising horses in the country boroughs was given to men like the Earl of Leicester. This tactic was of some help but landowners were generally recalcitrant, presenting all kinds of excuse to avoid having to find horses for the Queen's service. Cornish landowners suggested the country was unsuitable for the breeding of strong mares and to muster about 350 horses out of a county like Essex was like getting blood out of a stone. Little action seems to have been taken against landowners who did not even bother to answer the request. The horse seems to have been valued very poorly in the latter half of the sixteenth century.

Even at a time of great fear of an expected Spanish invasion, William Cecil, Chief Minister to Elizabeth, hoping to man all his defences, raised an army of 30,000 men, of which only 3,000 were horsemen.

Charles I had no greater success in mustering quality horses from the counties. His orders, in 1628 and 1629, that fighting horses be gathered in five parts of the country for his personal inspection caused an upsurge of alarm. Such was the volume of complaint that Charles was forced to abandon his scheme for establishment of an élite corps that would set a standard. With the decline of heavy cavalry and of emphasis on the tournament, with the wider use of armament and the decline in the use of armour, the breeding, stabling and care of the quality war-horse had fallen out of fashion. When light horses were eventually furnished by the counties, they were often poor, neglected, thin specimens, more fit for the knacker's yard than for the battlefield.

The demise of the heavy horse

But other factors were influencing and redirecting the role of the horse in war. The development of

Despite the rapidly changing style of warfare, the heavily armoured knight remained a feature of European warfare for many decades. In 1525, at the overwhelming French defeat at Pavia, the heavy cavalry was still in evidence.

The sixteenth-century
tournament was designed
as a purely ceremonial
occasion. The knights
would charge either into
single combat **top right** or
in a form of simulated
warfare **bottom right.**
Safety measures were also
taken to prevent the serious
injuries of previous times.
The lances were made to
shatter easily and saddles
were designed to enable the
rider to slide off the back
of the horse.

Far right The meeting of
Francis I and Henry VIII
on the Field of the Cloth
of Gold was designed, by
the ostentatious and lavish
pomp of both kings, to
show their respective
strength. However, much
to Henry's chagrin, this
meeting merely demons-
trated the superiority of
the French horses over the
English.

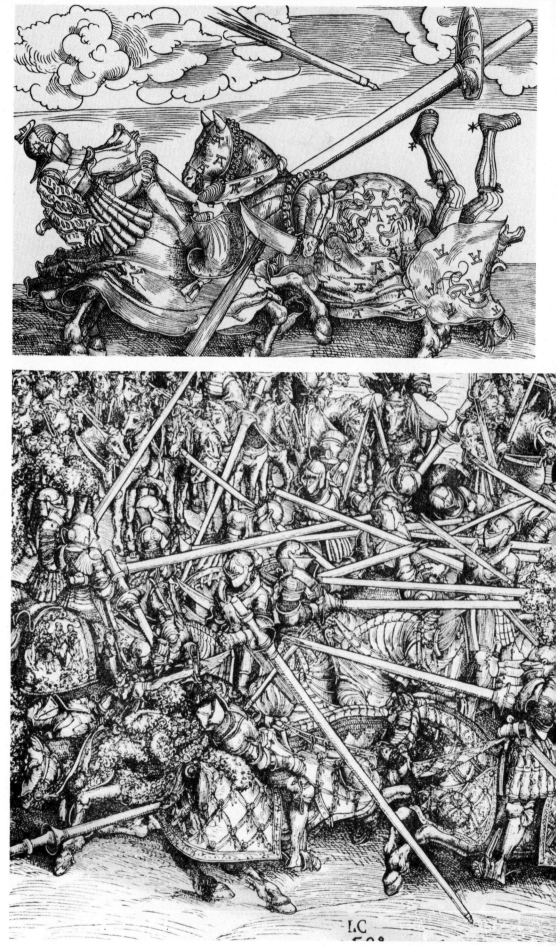

the long pike made a major impact on the battle-fields of sixteenth century Europe. This formidable weapon, when massed before advancing horses, presented a picket line of razor-sharp blades, which horses were unable to penetrate. The result was that the heavy charge of massed horsemen began to be abandoned.

A further disincentive to the use of the heavy horse was the growing use of powder and shot in battle, with consequent danger to the horse. The pageantry and wealth always associated with the horse began to undergo a subtle metamorphosis with the appearance of gunpowder. However magnificent a rider might appear, however expensive or beautiful the horse, they were no match for an ordinary infantryman armed with a musket.

Gustavus Adolphus

Gradually, the tactics of the horsemen were forced to change, due largely to the work of Gustavus Adolphus, King of Sweden (1594–1632). Gustavus had managed to persuade six regiments of Scottish soldiers to join his army under the Duke of Hamilton. The Scots had long been past-masters of the art of fighting on horseback: their iron discipline of horse and rider, and Gustavus' flair and imagination in the deployment of fast-moving riders, formed an unbeatable combination. It was Gustavus' boast that 5000 horsemen answered and responded when he moved his own reins. Such precision was unanswerable at the time, and in 1630, within eight months, the Swedish king had taken 80 fortresses with the unique nature of his cavalry discipline. Such was the zeal, the organization and the terror this general and his horsemen inspired at the battle of Lützen against the famous general Wallenstein, that although Gustavus was killed, his was the victory.

Below *A Yeoman of the Guard to Elizabeth I. Throughout this period there was an increasing difficulty in procuring enough horses of quality in England to amass an adequate fighting force.*

Below right *The Swiss pikemen formed an almost impenetrable defence making the vulnerability of the horse only too apparent in the early sixteenth century.*

Gustavus opened the battle, as was his wont, to the sound of music, his massed army singing Luther's hymn 'Ein Feste Burg Ist Unser Gott'. He led the first charge in person, killing the first of the enemy with his lance. While heading the second charge against the enemy's cavalry, he was struck by a shot from behind which killed him. Duke Bernard of Weimar cried out to the Swedes that the king had been made a prisoner, inflaming them to such a degree that nothing could resist the onslaught of the horses. There was terrible carnage and the enemy was forced to retreat before the irresistible waves of Swedish horsemen. The king was dead; he was, as rumour suggested, probably assassinated from behind by his cousin, the Duke of Saxe-Lauenburg. However, the fame of Gustavus Adolphus travelled far, and most of the great horsemen of the seventeenth century owe a debt of gratitude to him.

John Sobieski

Gustavus's tactics of feint and assault were employed to great effect by John Sobieski, a man who once served as a horseman bodyguard in the service of Louis XIV of France. His early training as a soldier was against the Cossacks, the Tartars and later the Russians: the finest horsemen of the known world gave him an extraordinary insight into the capability of the war-horse. Sobieski was to show, as history had shown so many times

before, that imaginative use of horses seemed inevitably to bring victory.

In 1667, Sobieski, with only 20,000 men, defeated 100,000 Tartars by a flanked cavalry manoeuvre that routed his enemy. Later, he defeated the Pasha of Damascus, who was leading an army of 200,000 men. Sobieski, with 10,000 horsemen, harried them into defeat. In 1683, he defeated the army of Kara Mustapha, driving the Turks across Hungary with the savagery of his pursuit. He even fought one of his victories in a snowstorm, his horses fanning like silent white ghosts across the snow-covered wastes to take the enemy by surprise. In the stables of Louis XIV, Sobieski had learned the growing skills of breeding from Arabic strains; breeding for wind and endurance as well as for speed. When he was made King of Poland, he spent great amounts of his own money setting up quality stables and horse-training schools.

It was the growing emphasis on the breeding of fine horses at stud that made the seventeenth century one of the most important in the improvement of the general standard of horses that could be used in battle, for defence or for display, such as the return of Charles II of England, when 20,000 horses lined his triumphant route.

The growth of expertise

One of the first great experts of the time was the

Below *John Sobieski, the saviour of Vienna from the final westward thrust of the Turks, learnt much from Gustavus.*

Above *It was the Swedish cavalry which delivered the knock-out blow at Breitenfeld. They were armed with both sword and pistols but the sword was much the dominant weapon with the pistol held in reserve.*

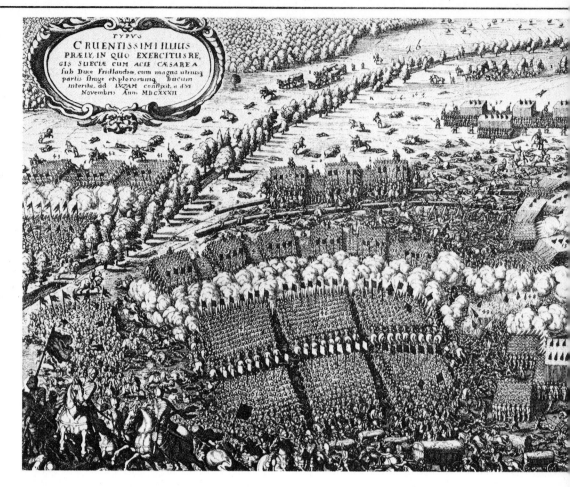

Duke of Newcastle, who was one of the greatest trainers and breeders of horses England has ever had. After the Civil War, Newcastle, like many other Royalists, went abroad, where he founded a horse circus in Antwerp. While he was there, he wrote in 1658 a book called *A General System of Horsemanship*. Despite being poor in exile, he still managed to buy quality horses. Newcastle was a great believer in the mixed English breeds for military purposes, and, as he records, the cost of a fine Arab horse could be anything between £500 and £3000. He returned to England in 1660 to become equestrian tutor to Charles II, whom he had taught from early childhood.

There had been other men who appreciated the significance of the horse in the defence of the realm. Sir Edward Harwood petitioned Charles I, warning the king of the decline in the numbers of great war-horses in the country. He did not believe that as many as 2000 could be found in the whole country. He went to great lengths to point out that French horses were superior to English in equal combat. He blamed the indifference of the nobility to the raising of military horses, when they were prepared to spend fortunes on racing animals.

Despite the interest and enthusiasm of such men, the general attitude towards the raising and breeding of horses in England was lamentable, and it was the prime cause of successive monarchs' difficulties in mustering large numbers of quality horses. Horses that were kept and trained in the few existing established Horse Schools (Manèges) lived to the age of 25 without losing their suppleness. The Duke of Newcastle had pointed out that the exercise of the manège was 'to supple a horse and put him upon his haunches, both which do mightily preserve him'. This position of the horse, set back upon his haunches, was very popular with trainers of the period; certainly many paintings of horses of the seventeenth century depict them with their weight back and their body tensed and powerful, like a great spring waiting to be unleashed.

Oliver Cromwell

Perhaps the most significant person to concern himself with the military exploitation of the horse was Oliver Cromwell. It is not unlikely that Cromwell had read of the glory of generals like Tamurlaine and Gustavus Adolphus; he certainly practised many of the methods of the former, and himself led his own men with the courage of the latter. It was not until he was 43 years old that he came to the position of power that was to give him the opportunity of developing into one of the finest cavalry leaders that Europe has produced. Until that time, he had been content to follow the occupation of country squire and to sit for the town of Cambridge in the English Parliament. He had no training as a general, though his life in the country had made him knowledgeable about horses.

It was Cromwell, for example, who was aware

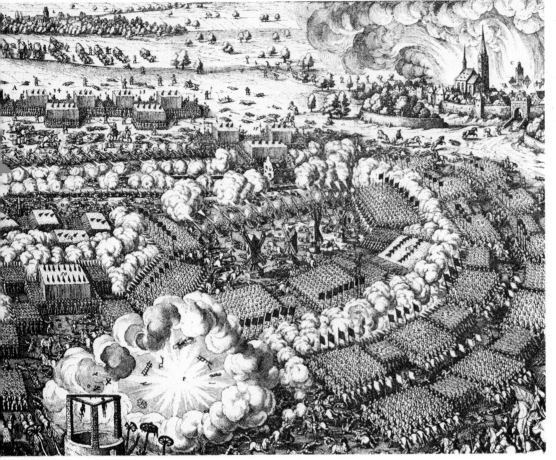

Left *The battle of Lutzen taken from the 'Theatrum Europaeum'. The horse at this time was being kept from the centre of the fray and used mainly as for sweeping actions on the fringes of the battle.*

Below left *An Imperialist army on the march. Armies at this time underwent a considerable increase in size. Without Gustavus Adolphus' strictly enforced discipline chaos would have ensued.*

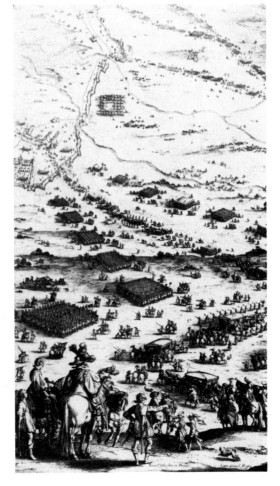

of the debilitating effect on the cavalry of using the old, slow coursers that had been so much in vogue in the time of Henry VIII. Seventeenth-century soldiers carried less armour (in fact, it was going out of fashion rapidly) and it was natural that a commander of genius should have seen the relationship between the speedy Arab horse, whose merits had been known since 1300 BC, and the active, mobile soldier of the mid-seventeenth century. In 1648, Cromwell confiscated all the fine Arab and oriental stock from Sir John Fenwick, stud master to Charles I. The Tutbury Royal stud was dispersed and many of its finest Arabs sent to Ireland for crossing with Irish pony strains.

At the beginning of the Civil War, Cromwell was commissioned as a captain in the cavalry arm of the Parliamentary army. He commanded close to 100 horsemen and other non-commissioned officers. Perhaps the strongest element of the Parliamentary forces was the collection of eastern counties centred on Cambridge and known as the Eastern Association. These men were the hard core of the opposition to Charles, and their courage, moulded by the moral fervour and religious discipline of Cromwell, was to prove an invincible combination.

The man most fitted to oppose Cromwell as a master of horse during the English Civil war was the nephew of Charles I, Prince Rupert. Rupert had a taste for military glory and was experienced in European military tactics, besides being a born

cavalry officer and a leader of courage and imagination. The armies of Gustavus Adolphus provided the example that Rupert followed. His principal use of the horse in battle was the close shock charge, with sabre raised for cutting and hacking; once the enemy had been scattered, they were pursued with heavy pistol. It was the charge that was ultimately to prove Rupert's undoing. His men tended to be aristocratic and haughty, though there is no question that they were brave and loyal. Having made their initial charge, they tended to lose the effectiveness of their grouping; they dissipated their energies in wild pursuits, often for personal gain, among the enemy baggage; they separated and exhibited a lack of the discipline that Cromwell was to see and use as the cohesive force of his own cavalry. Rupert was like fire: he burned, incandescent, during the first moments of battle, but soon lost his intensity.

In the early part of the war, Rupert's shock tactics enabled him to win a number of engagements, at Cirencester, Hereford and Lichfield, but at Worcester, Edgehill and Chalgrove Field he was remarkable more for his courage and dashing opportunism than for his military strategy. The king still believed in Rupert's abilities and made him general of the Royalist forces but his blunders at Naseby were one of the most important factors in the defeat and subsequent execution of the king.

In his first commission in the cavalry, Cromwell applied his ideas of discipline to making a model army that would be superior to any other. Like other generals of vision, he made sure that he had spies in the Royalist ranks; he learned both from them and from his own observation about the techniques of the Royalist armies. He soon became one of the greatest cavalry leaders England had produced. In ten years, between 1642, when he founded the defensive bands for the city of Cambridge, and 1652, when he became commander-in-chief, he remodelled, inspired and disciplined with an iron hand the army that was in effect the first standing army that England had ever possessed. Cromwell had seen the effectiveness of Rupert to the Royalist cause, and though he was aware of the power of the ordinary soldier, when disciplined and ordered, he was nevertheless aware of the imaginative possibility of the horse and its power to decide a battle by its speed and effectiveness.

In the last resort, however, the use of horses in battle has always been in relation to other significant details. It was useless to pit horses against pikes or to expose them to the relentless pounding of artillery or the sniping of muskets. The horse had to receive the maximum of protection, to be held significantly in reserve, not brazed against enormous odds. It was this capacity for organizing details that singled out Cromwell as a great general. His capacity for minutiae was, like Napoleon's, enormous and the leadership qualities of both were built on Francis Bacon's dictum that 'knowledge is power'.

Above *An illustration from the early pages of Newcastle's famous work showing a 'Paragon un Barbe'. The influence of interbreeding was beginning to be recognized at this time.*

Left *Sir Thomas Fairfax, general of the Parliamentary forces.*

Below left *The Royalist Duke of Newcastle. It was during his exile that he evolved his ideas on equitation.*

Opposite page *The charge of Prince Rupert's cavalry at Edgehill, the first pitched battle of the English civil war, in 1642. With his usual impetuosity, Rupert squandered the initial impetus by continuing the pursuit for three miles.*

Cromwell's army was founded upon the principle of simple piety, free from vice and coarseness, and no plundering or drinking was allowed. Having chosen quality officers, he tried also to supply them with the best possible horses. He tried to make certain that his men did not weigh down their horses with unnecessary accoutrements. He saw speed and manoeuvrability as the two great essences of horse warfare. Cromwell's horses were always well looked after, and he it was who founded the principle of the soldier caring for, feeding and protecting his own horse. Horse and rider were in concert: each depended upon the other. If the horse failed, the man was next to useless. It was this care for detail that turned Cromwell's military horses into some of the most disciplined seen upon a battlefield. Their formation, control and attack were superior to anything to be seen in the Royalist armies.

In 1651, Cromwell served his last occasion as a soldier in the field at the Battle of Worcester. After crossing the Severn, he defeated the Royalist forces and took over 10,000 prisoners. It was the last great battle of a civil war that had raged for seven long years. Cromwell, who had begun as a captain of horse, ended his career with the rank of commander-in-chief. In the words of Von Hoenig, the Prussian military writer, Cromwell was the greatest general England ever produced and the greatest cavalry leader of any nation at any time.

Once he became Protector, Cromwell began to build up the quality of horses in England; perhaps to make sure that the power of the army would in future rest upon an adequate supply of superior horses. He made energetic attempts to import Arabian horses into the country to improve the bloodstock. While Cromwell's ambassador Lockhart was in France, he was presented with four beautiful Arab saddle horses by Cardinal Mazzarin. It was a gift that greatly pleased the Protector.

Cromwell finally dispensed with the last of the heavy horses or destriers. His own experience told him that the future did not lie with armour-clad men sitting upon giant horses from Flanders, but with the sleek animals of the East. He had agents and horse buyers combing the Mediterranean to buy Arab horses.

Charles II

But, as Shakespeare wrote, 'the whirlygig of time brings in his revenges'. Within an hour of his restoration in 1660, following Cromwell's death in 1658, Charles II had seized Cromwell's Arab stud and the order went forth: 'forthwith seize all the goods of such persons as sate as Judges upon the late King, and such other horses as are seized of or belonging to such persons be carried to the Mews, for the service of his Majesty'.

The return of Charles II heralded a reign in which enormous sums of money were spent on importing the very finest oriental mares and stallions. Sometimes, the annual expenditure on horses reached £17,000. These Royal Mares, as they came to be known, together with their off-spring, laid the foundation for the best of British bloodstock to come. Having got the best of horses, Charles was able to mount some of his own personal regiments on matching steeds for ceremonial parades and for personal protection. He called them the Household Cavalry and they consisted of the Life Guards, the Royal Horse Guards and the King's Dragoon Guards. The continued crossing of foreign with English breeds was to encompass a greater number of horses, although the merits of the native breeds ought not to be overlooked. A certain Dr Fuller, writing in 1662, noted:

'Our English horses have in a mediocre degree all the necessary good properties. . . . For stature and strength of middle size and are both seemly and serviceable, and while the seller praiseth them too much, and the buyer too little the unbiased bystander will give them due consideration'.

But perhaps the finest picture of horses at the close of the seventeenth century came from Langbaine, in 1685. Describing the export of oriental horses, he writes: 'Some merchants affirm that there cannot be a more noble sight to a lover of horses than to walk into pastures near Constantinople about sailing time, when he may see many hundred gallant horses tethered and every horse has his attendant or keeper, with his little tent plac'd near him to lie in that he may look to him and take care to shift him to fresh grass as occasion requires; the Price of a Turk is commonly £100 or £150 a horse, and when bought it is difficult to get a pass'.

Opposite page *Cromwell at Marston Moor. Although an inexperienced commander, Cromwell soon evolved his own ideas on the use of the horse in battle, speed and manoeuvrability being the nodal points for his strategy.*

Left *Training with the right hand in front of Newcastle's Welbeck Manor.*

The rise of schooling

Marlborough gleaned many of his ideas from Gustavus, believing highly trained and efficient horsemen would serve him far better than the indisciplined rabble that constituted many European armies.

The eighteenth century was known as the Age of Reason, but in military terms it was a time when the great states of Europe—England, France, Prussia, Austria and Russia—were settling the principal areas of their frontiers and battling to maintain the precarious balance of power. Artillery was being developed, carbine and bayonet were replacing the pike and infantry was again coming to the fore in the battle plans of generals.

The seventeenth century, of course, had begun the great interest in horse-training and management. In 1717 was published a book called *The Complete Horseman*, written by the Sieur de Solleysell, equerry to the French king. The book is a manifesto of the kinds of idea then in circula-

tion about the care and training of horses, especially by the military. We are told that Italians were the first to write down detailed training programmes designed to master the horse by art instead of brutality:

'So it was that all the French, and other nations, went to Italy to be taught, the centre for the finest horsemanship being first at Naples, and later at Rome, to which great numbers of all peoples went to make themselves horsemen. But those whose first wish was to reach the greatest degree of perfection in this art, went to Naples, where they were kept two or three years before the Masters'.

The origin of such establishments, as of many schools of philosophy in the East, was the desire of some men to perfect a small area of human endeavour; in this instance, the control of a horse. The men, many of them serving officers, who attended such schools would carry with them and disseminate the ideas they had absorbed. They soon learned that horses that were supple and free-moving as a result of their exercises would serve them that much better when used in warfare. The relationship between well-trained men on well-trained horses and success in battle was quickly noted. Horse-training schools became bigger and the finest teachers were often brought in by individual monarchs.

The Duke of Marlborough

The first great cavalry leader of the century was the Duke of Marlborough, whose deeds of glory were to be rewarded by Queen Anne with the gift of Blenheim Palace to commemorate his great victory at Blenheim in 1704. At the opening of the War of the Spanish Succession, there were scarcely 15 regiments of horses in England, Scotland and Ireland; and those regiments were quite

The French cavalry, in contrast to the English and their allies, used the gun as their main weapon, even in close combat.

small and ill-equipped. Since Elizabethan times, Parliament and public opinion had been against the idea of a standing army. Suspicious of the potential political ascendancy of a standing army, people had long preferred that men and horses should be banded together only when danger threatened. But, as William of Orange tried to show at the end of the seventeenth century, dependable regular regiments of infantry and cavalry were essential. Gradually, Parliament voted the necessary money to buy horses and tackle and, by the time of the Battle of Blenheim, Marlborough was able to put eight English cavalry squadrons into the field, and to match that with eight of foreign mercenaries.

John Churchill, Duke of Marlborough, was born in 1650 of an old Cavalier family who had suffered much in the Civil War. He joined a regiment of footguards at the age of 16 and soldiered in the campaigns in Holland between 1672 and 1677. He learned the art of cavalry deployment under such brilliant horsemen as Condé, Vauban, and Turenne, and later learned to perfect the art, first against the Duke of Monmouth's rebellion, when Churchill commanded a regiment of dragoons, and then against the Irish horsemen, under Dominic Sheldon, in 1699. It was William III who granted Churchill his Earldom of Marlborough.

Marlborough's qualities, like those of Cromwell before him, were principally qualities of spirit and enterprise. He believed passionately in the qualities of the horsemen and his ability to influence battles. He was, for example, a great believer in the idea of the general as exemplar. He made sure that he rose at the same time as his cavalrymen; his quarters were among theirs when they encamped before battle, and he endured the common hardship they suffered in the pursuit of their goals.

In view of the circulation of ideas about horses, both before and during the lifetime of the Duke of Marlborough, it is not surprising to find him putting forward many intelligent and practical principles as a basis for the training of the complete horse-soldier and, through him, the dynamic of the mounted troop. His first rule was that horse and man were one. Together, they meant something; and if that union of man and horse were expressed with perfect symmetry and discipline and could be moulded into larger units under perfect control, there would be no limit to what could be achieved. To achieve this end, Marlborough contrived detailed exercises, based on the work of the Duke of Newcastle, to make his cavalry the finest in Europe.

The War of the Spanish Succession gave the opportunity for the full flowering of Marlborough's genius with cavalry. After the campaigns in Holland in 1703, he made his great march to the Danube. Marlborough encouraged his cavalrymen to have great pride in themselves and in their horses. His first insistence was upon care of the horse, and maintenance of the equipment. It was his contention that the quartering of the horses was as important as the quartering of the men. He himself set the example that or-

ganization underlay victory. On the famous march to the field of Blenheim, Marlborough and the cavalry travelled a few days ahead of the main army, reconnoitring and keeping in close formation.

In the summer of 1704, when Prince Eugene of Savoy saw Marlborough's cavalry for the first time, he commented on the quality of the animals, the standard of discipline and the extraordinary spirit of the men. The English cavalry were mounted principally upon black coursers, bred by William III especially for war and in particular for those tactical contingencies that always seemed to arise in the deployment of cavalry wings in set-piece battle strategies. The units had been trained by Marlborough to fight as one. Their initial attacks were based on the technique of the shock charge; but instead of dissipating the initial charge, they were able to branch and wheel and use secondary flanking attacks in a completely disconcerting manner.

After completing his astonishing march to the Danube in 1704, Marlborough crossed the river under the guns of Schullenberg, a feat of the most brilliant daring. He then, with the assistance of another great cavalry leader, Prince Eugene, defeated Tallard, Marshal of France, and the Elector of Bavaria at the Battle of Blenheim. This decisive blow against the power of Louis XIV was followed in quick succession by victories at Ramilles in 1706, Oudenarde in 1708 and Malplaquet in 1709; where, despite the foolish blunders of William III's son, the Prince of Orange (who precipitately and without orders led his reserve cavalry force into battle, nearly bringing about Marlborough's defeat), Marlborough deployed his cavalry with an ingenuity and imagination that Napoleon himself admired and indeed used in his own great victory at Austerlitz in 1805.

Compared with Marlborough's achievements, the use of horses by the military in Europe (with the possible exception of Frederick the Great and Napoleon) during the next 100 years, was of a very poor order—at times, reduced to almost comic extremes. The story is related of the Battle of Dettingen in 1743, which was fought against the French. George II led the English troops together with his son, the Duke of Cumberland.

After a disastrous handling of the cavalry, the horses of the king and the duke bolted, frightened by a sudden burst of musket fire. The two animals galloped off in opposite directions. The king's horse ran through his own army towards the rear, the duke's horse carried his master almost into the French lines, where he received a small but painful leg wound. The king returned to battle without his horse; even if his horsemanship was poor, his courage proved to be a very high order.

Again, at Culloden in 1745, when the same Duke of Cumberland was putting down the insurgent Scots clansmen, his use of cavalry against a disorganized enemy force proved to be clumsy and, in the last resort, unethical; in no sense a measure of what was possible from an imaginative leader.

After the Stuart rebellion of 1745, real efforts were made to re-structure British cavalry regiments and especially to raise a great number of dragoon horse regiments, who were more and more to be associated with light mounted military duties. Perhaps the most famous of these were the 17th Lancers, formed in 1759 (known as Annus Mirabilis, because of the many military and political victories in that year), who were to achieve fame as the 'Death or Glory Boys'.

Above *A rather unflattering portrait of Marlborough, one of the most outstanding commanders to grace the British battle scene.*

Left *An illustration taken from George II's Regimental Clothing Book to show the uniform of the First Life guards. Uniforms had been slowly evolving since the English civil war.*

Opposite page *Hans Joachim von Zeiten. The ability of this general was to help make the Prussian army one of the most efficient and feared in Europe.*

Von Seydlitz and Von Zeithen

In the middle years of the century, Frederick the Great of Prussia, with his famous generals, von Seydlitz and von Zeithen, were to carry forward the qualities of horsemanship and control that had distinguished the Duke of Marlborough.

Frederick learned about the quality of cavalry in the disastrous Battle of Mollwitz, fought in 1741. A sudden charge of Austrian cavalry completely shattered the Prussian lines and sent him, surrounded by his ruined cavalry, headlong from his first battle. The Prussians appeared to have no answer to the tactics of the Austrian horsemen: first, the heavy charge towards the enemy, pistols fired from the saddle; then a stroke with a sabre, sharp as a razor, at the head of the enemy's horse; and finally a backward slash at the rider as they hurtled past. They were brilliantly effective, but, even as his horse carried him from the field, Frederick was marking down the experience for his future education.

Yet, despite the disaster of the horse and the fact that the king had been driven from the field, the Prussian infantry won the day. Frederick described it as 'one of the rudest battles fought within the memory of man'. The painful memory of his indisciplined horse was to remain with him all his life. But in June 1745, the new Prussian cavalry displayed a courage and quality that scattered the Austrians like chaff before the wind. At the Battle of Hohenfriedberg, more than 60 Austrian standards were captured by one regiment of Prussian dragoons alone. Frederick informed his mother: 'So decisive a defeat has not been since Blenheim'.

Frederick II congratulates von Seydlitz after the battle of Zorndorf. Ignoring the king's impatient demands, Seydlitz proved his ability by gaining an overwhelming victory.

The architect, however, of Frederick's mature victories, such as the ones at Rossbach and Zorndorf, was the great horseman General von Seydlitz. He was not simply a master tactician on the field; he was also a superlative trainer of horse and horsemen. Seydlitz was in the great tradition of men who school horses: an intuitive rider, well-read and well-informed about horse-care and husbandry, he was possessed of that kind of intelligence that originates new method. Moreover, like both Cromwell and Marlborough before him, his successes were due directly to the quality and thoroughness of his training.

Seydlitz thought of the cavalryman as the complete horseman: rider, friend, sustainer, trainer and veterinarian. The performance of the horse was directly related to the qualities of the man who was its rider. He taught his men to break and ride any horse, and to ride that horse over any terrain. He inculcated self-discipline into the rider. To difficult and precise elements of horse-control, he added a majestic orchestration of weapon use to supplement the advantage that intelligent and ingenious manipulation of the horse would bring. The quality of his own swordsmanship was legendary; one feat he is reputed to have perfected was the splitting with his sabre of an apple one of his men had thrown into the air while he was at full gallop.

Before the Battle of Rossbach, in 1757, Seydlitz, who was junior to many of the generals present, was placed in full command of all the cavalry by Frederick. The faith of his monarch was fully justified, for von Seydlitz, who was to become known as the Prince of Dragoons, devastated the enemy flank and pursued them for miles from the field of battle.

Again, at the Battle of Zorndorf, in August 1758, the matchless von Seydlitz revealed not only his wonderful discipline of horse and man but also qualities of character that singled him out. When told to advance with his cavalry upon the Russian gun emplacements, he refused the king's orders twice. At the third command, Frederick informed him: 'After the battle you will answer for it with your head.' 'Sire,' answered the imperturbable Seydlitz, 'After the battle my head will be at the service of the king.' He then justified his previous reticence by making two pincer charges at the time that he considered most judicious. Once again, his qualities of timing and organization proved successful, and his delighted king preferred embracing him to beheading him. It was extraordinary that such deeply entrenched infantry positions could have been routed by cavalry, but that is what Seydlitz achieved.

In 1759, at Kunersdorf, the king again gave Seydlitz orders to advance in very dangerous circumstances. Again, von Seydlitz's instinct told him to refuse. The king, however, was adamant and eventually the cavalry went forward against the Russian might. Von Seydlitz was wounded and his superb squadrons of horse decimated by cannon and musket, without the gaining of an inch of ground.

Frederick, carried from the field by his own hussars, was almost beside himself with rage and anguish; his character was not the kind to accept defeat with philosophical calm. Four days later, however, his spirit returned, when he found that the Allies had not followed up their victory.

At the Battle of Liebnitz, in 1760, von Zeithen, a young cavalry commander in the mould of von Seydlitz, made his mark, the first of many. And although the Prussians were victorious, the departure from the field, as related by a young lieutenant called Archenholtz, indicates with great clarity the horrors of war for man and horse.

'This army, spent with bloody toil and girt by mighty hosts, must press on without rest and without delay, and yet must bear with it every gun and man that had been taken and all the wounded as well. . . . Nothing was left behind, not a single wounded man, Prussian or Austrian, and at nine-o-clock, four hours after the end of the battle, the army with its enormous load was in full march'.

One might add that without the use of horses to carry wounded and baggage and survivors the Prussian army might have been totally lost.

The rise of horse schools

It became apparent in the eighteenth century that horses and riders trained in Haute Ecole were more effective in battle. The whole idea of the schools (which were never popular with the English) was to so order the behaviour of the horse that, without constricting him in any way, his natural movements and predilections would be noted and controlled with the minimum of external paraphernalia, a rein and bridle being enough to order and direct the forces of the horse's body and the manifestations of its intelligence. It was determined that the good schools would, with intelligent and kind practices, channel the horse's strength and beauty so that he, once ordered, would respond to the lightest hand of any rider. The art was in the ordering. Such were the broad principles on which the schools were founded, however, that the training of horses to encourage nobility, expertise and discipline inevitably involved the rider's considering his own relationship with the horse.

An interesting example of the kind of situation that could arise is seen in the case of Philip Astley, a sergeant-major in the 15th Light Dragoons in the mid-eighteenth century. The Astley family had long been famous for its expertise with horses, and Philip was no exception.

In 1768, he was demobilized and determined to carry on his career with horses, if possible, by setting himself up as a riding teacher to rich patrons and by giving exhibitions to raise money for a riding school. All Astley's writings on the subject of horsemanship exhibit a quality of perfection in matters of detail. His attitude to the horse was one of veneration; he placed very high

Opposite page above
The beneficial effects of training had really come to fruition by the mid-eighteenth century and Pluvinel's 'L'Instruction du Roy' was looked to for guidance, although many of the demands he made of the horse's strength were unkind and often almost impossible.

Opposite page below
Few really great commanders of ability arose in the middle part of the century and never was this so apparent as in the methods used to put down the second Jacobite rising.

Von Seydlitz before the
battle of Rosbach in 1757.
Few commanders were to
achieve his successes yet the
King's interference and
lack of confidence in his
ability were to lead to a
resounding defeat.

value on the skills of horse and rider, and his
greatest wish was to found a riding school of the
very highest standards. His exhibitions resulted
in his enormous popularity and as a result,
ironically, his exhibition hall became a famous
amusement centre for many years. His attitude to
the art of horsemanship, however, remained un-
changed. Astley's 'System of Equestrian Education, exhibiting the Beauties and Defects of the
Horse, with serious and important observations
of general excellence' reveals the tone of Astley's
ideas. His was an aristocratic view of the horse
and his descriptions signify his reverence and his
observation of the beauty of the horse in motion:

'The exercise of the horse reveals certain fine
manners, with grace, address and elegance,
joined to a perfect knowledge of the use, perfec-
fections and imperfections (discipline and com-
bats) of the horse and the purity of its actions. I
conceive the rider may be said to be in cadence
when his seat on horseback is strictly agreeable to
the eye: every corresponding action of the rider's

body, as well as the horse, may, if regular and
conformable to the pure art of equitation, be
called in cadence, similar to such measure regu-
lated in dancing'.

Such a quotation, coming as it does from an
ex-sergeant of dragoons, reveals the finesse and
standard of horsemanship that was often axio-
matic in the élite horse regiments. The qualities
of the techniques were to be found in the very
nature of their approach to the art of horsemanship. Also basic to any system of thorough horse-
management is the quality of humility that occurs
again and again in the finest captains of cavalry.

The most successful approach to military
horses appears to have been, paradoxically, the
human approach. Bearing in mind the fate of
millions of horses in times of war since man first
began to exploit them, it is significant that the
best and most effective horses to enter upon the
battlefields of the eighteenth century were often
those on whom the most loving care and attention
had been lavished in order to raise their discipline

to that standard where they cheerfully and instantly obeyed the orders of their masters, even if such instant response were to result in their immediate death.

Finally, perhaps one of the most significant changes in the pattern of horse deployment in war was to take place towards the close of the eighteenth century in the emerging colonies of America. There, over many years, the Indian population was learning to use horses with consumate skill and ability. There, George III's organized and disciplined armies, with centuries of tradition behind them, were to founder on skilful guerilla tactics. There, man used the horse to survive, to carry all his goods and to hunt for his very food. It is not surprising that training at such essential levels should have resulted in horsemen who were the equal of, and in most cases superior to, the formal military groups of George III's men. In many ways, the best military use of horses was often the most simple.

Napoleon—
"They must be seen to be destroyed"

The eighteenth century certainly saw a quite dramatic development in the size of armies, in the number of horses used in warfare, both for draught and combat duties, in the change of emphasis towards light rather than heavy cavalry and in the greater use of Arabian stock to improve and specialize animals for the horse regiments. With the possible exception of cavalry officers of genius, such as those fighting at the head of the armies of Frederick the Great, the average general cared little about detailed training for horse regiments, and was content to use his horsemen on the wings of infantry battalions, to forage or charge, as occasion demanded. Such perfunctory training was far from the standard demanded by one of the greatest military strategists the world has ever known: Napoleon Bonaparte.

France before the Revolution

A horse-loving nation for centuries past, France had been one of the first nations to set up horse schools and to concentrate on improving the country's stock by selective breeding. Louis XIV had founded the Haras du Pin, the most famous of the great French studs. Louis, a perfectionist, ensured that his cavalry was equipped with quality horses, developed especially to unite the power of the old tourney horses and the light but powerful animals that were becoming more popular and necessary as the century developed. As the use of armour became almost defunct, the horse became an incisive force, to be used with imagination and fluency in the great battles involving the principal nations of Europe. The new requirements were for reconnoitring, for feints, for communication, for doubling up as transport horses, for dragging artillery, and for use in a secondary manner as heavy cavalry. Napoleon was to devise new patterns of horse movement, both before and during battles; his expertise, his regard for the horse as a match-winning combination with artillery, was very high.

As the century progressed, the great natural areas of France, such as Orne, Normandy, Anjou and Navarre, were given over to the raising of brood mares and the development of great cavalry schools such as the one at Saumur, founded in the reign of Louis XV; and before the great Revolution of 1789, horse-breeding was centred in the west and southwest. These areas were on the most direct trading routes from the Arabian lands that supplied the finest mares and stallions. The difference between French and English quality horses had been noted at the

Napoleon at Austerlitz. Although an artillery officer by training, Napoleon was a master of co-ordinating the different arms of his forces, using each in their respective roles to gain the best possible results.

Field of the Cloth of Gold. It is not surprising to find an English veterinary surgeon named Osmer writing, in 1761: 'Arabian horses being better constituted for action than other horses do by means hereof excel all others. . . . The attachment of some men to what is commonly called "a good English horse", is as absurd as the objection of sportsmen to blood, i.e. cat-legged things'.

The attack on horsebreeding

On January 29, 1790, by decree, the Revolution suppressed all studs. Such foolishness was protested against by the army generals, and certainly by the statesman Mirabeau, who had studied horses in England. The leaders of the Revolution had issued the decree because of the financial strictures their excesses had brought about. In a couple of years, the thoughtless crusaders at the head of the country had, with fanatical zeal, set aside the worth of centuries. Realization quickly followed that a foolish act had been committed. So central were horses to the post-Revolutionary needs of the Republic that before all else was

restored in the national scene, studs were rebuilt and reorganized.

The situation was desperate. In the third year, a law was passed for the immediate establishment of seven stallion depots. In an atmosphere of intrigue, destruction and iconoclasm, it was difficult for something as seminal and peaceful as horse-breeding to be firmly established. By the sixth year, further measures had to be implemented.

It was largely due to the extraordinary feats of the cavalry at Stettin, in 1806, that Napoleon, who has been called the world's greatest cavalry leader, decided to reorganize breeding and attempt to restore some of the quality horses which had hitherto made up the bulk of the French cavalry.

'A good Arab stallion', said Napoleon, 'is the world's best horse; far better than the thoroughbred for improving all breeds'. Trying to replace the studs lost so recently, he obtained first-class Arab horses, to set the breeding tone for each of the establishments. He brought the Arab stud

from Deux Ponts in Bavaria to Pompadour in 1814, and it was revived later, in 1815. When he was on his abortive Egyptian campaigns, Napoleon took care to find some of the finest animals available and to ship them back to France. These animals included some from the exceptional and justly famous stock of Mohammed Ali; and the kind of animal chosen can be seen on the coin that was minted to celebrate the English victory in Egypt.

Problems of recruitment

If Napoleon was having difficulty with horses, then the English were having real problems in getting men to serve in the regiments of cavalry. There is interesting material to be discovered in the letters of a cavalry officer named Robert Long, who fought under Wellington in the Peninsular War. Advertisements for cavalry officers then were nothing if not exclusive:

'Only protestants and natives of Great Britain; no Apprentices, seamen, marines, militia men, colliers, stragglers, vagrants or possible deserters.

Recruits must be perfectly straight, well-featured, in every way well made and not heavy-limbed, not above thirty nor under seventeen (except any fine boy over 16). All recruits to undergo a medical examination to discover fits, rupture, broken bones, sore legs, scaled hands or running sores. Men over twenty to be not less than 5ft 7 ins in height'.

English horses, however, were beginning to show the results of the methods and techniques suggested by men like the Duke of Newcastle. The great work of the Duke had been followed up in the eighteenth century by the Earl of Pembroke, who published, in 1761, his famous: 'A method of Breaking Horses and Teaching Soldiers to ride, designed for the use of the Army'. The book was an attempt to put into print, for the service of all regiments, the painstaking research and intelligent observation of horse-lovers such as the Duke of Marlborough. Its detail and its closely argued philosophy of organization of men into cavalry units were to transform British horse regiments and encourage

the discipline and perseverance that was to mark the English cavalry at Waterloo:

'The lesson of reining back and piafing, is excellent to conclude with, and puts a horse well and properly on the haunches . . . for the piaffe in backing, is rather too much to expect in the hurry, which cannot but attend such numbers both of men and horses, as are obliged to be taught together in regiments. This lesson must never be attempted at all, till horses are very well supplied, and somewhat accustomed to be put together'.

Certain men were beginning to look upon the field of battle as a perfectly organized system of move and counter-move, using horse artillery and cavalry as the main points of focus around which the various tabloids of strategy would be structured.

The French Revolution had made a most serious break in the old European order of monarchical states; new and dangerous ideas began to disturb the very fabric of the established order. Once again, war was to bring to a focus those deeper intensities; but the kind of war had changed. The new patterns of warfare that were to emerge under the genius of Napoleon were early forms that, a century later, were to mature into the holocaust of total or world war.

Napoleon

From his time at the free military school at Brienne, Napleon had been interested in horses and in the tactics of such famous French leaders as Condé and Turenne. Although, later, he was to specialize as an artillery officer, there is no doubt that the appeal of war and battle brought with it for him the joy of using cavalry with imagination and insight.

One of his greatest attributes as a commander of the finest calibre, like Cromwell's before him, was the ability to pick the finest men to serve under him. Even more important, perhaps: Napleon saw himself in heroic proportions. His portraits show him on prancing steeds and cavorting war horses, his hair tousled and his eyes piercing, his sword arm raised, the reins held in classic pose: all symbolize the nobility he principally associated with his own actions; and how better to express the conquering general, the master cavalry tactician, than by depicting him upon the almost inevitable white Arab stallion? The horse, for Napoleon, was the finest expression of his attitude to war; swift, decisive, omnipotent.

The ideal of the French Revolutionaries was the Graeco-Roman period of antiquity. Napoleon inculcated into his men the ideas of Sparta. His own greatness was generated by the Revolution. He was to become First Consul, and later Emperor, and his armies carried eagle standards, as the Romans had, before them.

'They must be seen to be destroyed'

Napoleon used his cavalry in small, closely woven units, each with a captain of horse, who was answerable to the brigadier of horse, men such as Kellerman, Murat or Lefebvre-Desnouettes, acting under the direct command of Napoleon himself. Napoleon tended, in battle, to throw the whole weight of one element of his army against what he considered to be the weak links in the enemy. To this end, he established a complex system of horse spies, to gain essential and up-to-the-minute information about the enemy. This work was often done at night, the reconnoitring horsemen riding black mounts, with black accoutrements, their horses' hooves often muffled with felt to prevent them from being discovered. Napoleon, like the great Genghis Khan, knew that victory was founded upon information and communication. Some of the 20,000 documents and dispatches published by his nephew, Napoleon III, reveal the quality of the organizing mind of Napoleon Bonaparte, the general.

At the Jena campaign, Napoleon's instructions to Murat were explicit. At the beginning of the campaign, which decimated Prussia, Murat, with three cavalry squadrons, led the advance brigades. His instructions as to placing and position, even of dispatch-carrying outriders, had all been written down by Napoleon, together with questions of information about the towns of Saalfeld, Saalburg and Hof, which had to be answered, as follows:

1) Is communication possible between Saalfeld and Saalburg?
2) Is communication possible between Saalfeld and Hof?
3) Is communication possible between Lobenstein and Hof?
4) What are the roads like?
5) Are they fit for infantry, for cavalry and artillery?
6) What is the position of the enemy about Hof, about Saalburg, and above all on the main road to Leipzig?

We note, from that 'above all', the vision of Napoleon's strategy: nothing was left to chance. The light cavalrymen streamed back and forth between his headquarters and his advancing armies like the brain, sending and receiving continual messages to and from the extremities. These specially trained horsemen were the cornerstone on which Napleon's reputation was built. It is, perhaps, significant that, after the disastrous Russian campaign had destroyed almost all his horses, Napoleon, in the following year of 1813, was ineffective at Leipzig because of the quality of his horses, and the lack of reconnaissance soldiers.

A particular policy of Napoleon's was to pursue the enemy with his victorious cavalry, often, as at Jena, for hundreds of miles. Murat spent over three weeks pursuing and harassing the defeated Prussians. The scene was always, for Napoleon, a symbol of the power of his genius: the enemy, swept into confusion, broken and scattered, fleeing like innumerable leaves before a mighty wind. He was the great master of tactical pursuit. 'The

Napoleon as he liked to picture himself mounted on a spirited white Arab stallion, reflecting the energy and dynamism he generated in the Empire.

Above *Murat leading the charge at Jena. One of Napoleon's finest qualities as a leader was in choosing commanders of ability.*

Above centre *Napolean left his troops to get home as best they could and hurried home.*

enemy must not be allowed to reform,' he would say, when told that he was victorious on the field of battle. 'They must be seen to be destroyed.'

In order to achieve his success, Napoleon behaved with the kind of ruthlessness that seems to be second nature to all great leaders of men. It has been estimated that, between 1804 and 1814, nearly 4,000,000 people died as a result of Napoleon's campaigns. No-one, apparently, counted the horses; on the retreat from Russia, almost 40,000 horses were lost, many of them eaten by the starving and frozen remnants of Napoleon's army. Napoleon himself, as he had done once before in Egypt, preferred to leave the army behind while he made his own way back to France in relative comfort.

Haute école

Another timely factor that underlay Napoleon's

successes in battle was the development of riding techniques, principally at the centres of Haute Ecole, which grew in importance in France in the eighteenth century. These schools were run basically for the service of the rich and therefore secondarily and quite naturally for the cavalry regiments of the army.

In the French horse schools, especially, there was a comprehensive quality about the training of the horses which distinguished the French cavalry throughout the eighteenth century. Their horses were schooled in what has come to be called dressage, but which in England might be called training. Significantly, the emphasis in France was not only on physical development but also on what might be called the horse's character or disposition. Gymnastic exercises enabled the horse to adjust to the unnatural weight of the rider on his back while keeping his balance and

providing him with the methods of quick recovery should he be forced to manoeuvre awkwardly or suddenly. The horses were taught changes of pace, alteration of stride and variation in the leading foreleg. They were taught the pirouette, a most difficult, almost circus-like movement of turning on the haunches, from the canter and at the canter, the horse pivoting on its hind legs while those legs continued cantering on the spot; a manoeuvre particularly useful to a fine swordsman. They also learned the passage and piaffe, two movements based on a cadenced high-stepping trot in which the horse assumed an architectural and controlled line. Such movements combined elegance and discipline, essential in the confusion and noise of battle. To bring a horse to the right degree of excellence might take as long as two years.

French horses of the middle and late eighteenth century were particularly well-trained in dressage with emphasis on the requirements of the cavalry. Cavalry were of prime importance in battle, and hand-to-hand encounters formed a large part of the known tactics. Consequently, horses were made so supple and responsive that they could be turned on a sixpence, horse and rider matching each other perfectly in rhythm and balance. The horse was generally balanced on his quarters, which was done by raising the head and neck as much as possible. The French verb for this short-rein control was 'dresser', from which came the noun, dressage. As cavalry conditions changed, with the development of shot and shell, so the schools responded to new needs and conditions. Many of the cavalry manuals of equitation of Napoleon's time contain the different methods extolled by the individual schools. The cavalry books often deal with the basic and necessary

Top *A French cavalryman in 1806.*

Above *In 1812 Napoleon made a rare but disastrous mistake. The invasion of Russia evolved into a tragic farce as this cartoon entitled 'Boney returning from Russia covered with glory leaving his army in COMFORTABLE Winter Quarters' shows.*

training of average horses and their riders; following this up with detailed training of groups and files of horsemen. It was most important, for example, for riders to be able to do simple things well in the cruel vicissitudes of war. It was not surprising, however, that different countries used different methods of training. The methods generally reflected the natural characteristics of the men of the country, incorporating such elements as courage, bravado, finesse, restraint or impetuosity. An asceticism about French horses and horsemen distinguished them from others, as if the rational element, so much a part of the French character, had manifested itself in the training of their horses.

Using well-trained cavalry on disciplined horses, Napleon rode to victory after victory. His heavy cavalry, which contained horsemen sometimes known as Cuirassiers on account of their helmets and breast plate armour, were an awesome sight in the charge. They practised, with swords sharp enough to sever a falling silk scarf, until they were expert. They could cut or thrust, confident in the knowledge that their horses could accommodate themselves to the changing fortunes of the swordsman and not lose balance.

Napoleon organized several cavalry schools, and picked certain officers and men to form the élite corps of cavalry he planned for the future. In 1805, when he threatened invasion of England and his army lay at Boulogne, he increased the number of his mounted soldiers from 60,000 to over 100,000. Of these, 22,000 were kept under the personal control of Napoleon himself and were led by one of his finest subordinates, General Murat. This cavalry reserve was to prove its worth on many occasions when Napoleon was in difficulties. When the invasion of England was postponed, the army moved to Austria, where General Murat was given the kind of explicit instructions that enabled Napoleon's generals to act decisively and well. On October 2, 1805,

Napoleon's dispatch to Murat read:

'You will protect my flank as I move obliquely to the Danube, which is a delicate operation. If the enemy intends to take the offensive, I must be warned in time to take action, and not be obliged to conform to that of the enemy'.

Later, at Wertingen, Murat, with three cavalry divisions, routed an Austrian army, taking over 2000 prisoners. This move enabled Napoleon to engage General Mack at Ulm, where Mack was forced to capitulate.

Thus Napoleon moved inexorably forward; and wherever he fought, the exploits of his horses and cavalrymen figure large in his dispatches: at Austerlitz, at Averstadt, in the Peninsular War, in Russia and even in defeat at Waterloo. He thought his misfortune at Waterloo largely due to his weakness in cavalry. His reconnaissance forces were depleted and thus failed to send him vital information concerning the whereabouts of the Prussian army under Blucher. Furthermore, his heavy cavalry broke in vain about the ironsquares of Wellington's infantry groups.

Throughout his military career, Napleon was a consummate craftsman where the cavalry were concerned. He had unbounded faith in his horses and men. But he had no fixed doctrine; he was as spontaneous as each day's new set of circumstances. He wrote: 'Cavalry charges are equally effective at the beginning, in the middle, and at the end of a battle.' At the same time, one of his favourite tactics was to keep a strong unit of cavalry in reserve, and to use it with devastating precision when the enemy was most tired. His planning and organization testify to his regard for the power of mounted troops. In 1806, the proportion of horsemen to foot-soldiers was in the ratio of one to five; he raised it to one to three. In all his great triumphs, Napoleon's consciousness of the military potential of the trained horse and soldier was central to his planning and ultimately to his achievements.

Below *Napoleon had many horses trained for war—it is said that he had eighteen shot from under him—but one had a career as long and colourful as his master. Brought to France after Aboukir Bay, Marengo, a small, grey Arab, was present at all the major campaigns of the Empire, surviving the harsh Russian campaign, and being captured at Waterloo at the age of twenty-two. He was then kept in England until his death at the age of thirty-eight.*

America-
The essential military horse

George Washington, the first great general to emerge at the outbreak in 1775 of the American War of Independence, had earlier fought in the Indian Wars. His experience of so dangerous and elusive an enemy as the Indian was to prove invaluable.

The introduction of the horse
The misnomer 'Indian' was first applied to the American native by Columbus, who, on reaching islands off the North American coast in 1492, assumed he had arrived at his intended destination, the Eastern Indian islands. It used to be thought that Columbus and subsequent explorers brought into Central and North America the first mares and stallions, later to multiply and be tamed and used by the Indians; recent archaeological evidence, however, suggests that primitive species of horse may have been numerous there as long ago as 50,000 years. The year of Columbus' landing marked the beginning of the end for the native Central and North American. From that time, the reasoning power and cupidity of 'civilized' Europe were ranged against the instinct and innocence of a primitive people. Over the next four centuries, the Indians were to be exploited, cheated, killed; their homelands and nationhood were to be cruelly torn from them.

During the 50 years after Columbus' discovery, Spanish explorers invaded Peru and most of Central America. In 1540, Francisco Vasquez de Coronado led 250 mounted soldiers and about 4000 friendly Indian carriers, on foot, into the desert and scrubland northeast of the Gulf of California. Any Indians encountered en route were terrorized by the Spanish guns and the 'monsters' the soldiers rode. In two years, Coronado, his avaricious dreams fed by Indian legends of cities of gold and silver, explored almost to the border of present-day Nebraska before turning southward again in angry disillusion. The native tribes of the southwest were the first of the Indians to suffer the rapacious greed of the new White Lords from over the water.

The Spaniards were the first to make the horse an instrument of war in North America. They used it as a draught animal, too, and for controlling herds of cattle, which had also come with the Spaniards. The Indian was not slow to learn. The horse was to become his greatest ally in the pursuit of food and war.

When the Spanish Empire began to falter, the French and the English continued the colonization and exploitation of North America. The French appear to have had a better relationship than other conquerors with the Indians; French and Indian fought together against the English on several occasions.

It seems likely that, despite his awareness of its advantages, the Indian was prevented by successive invaders from using the horse. No doubt it was realized that, mounted, the Indian might prove a terrifying adversary. When the Indians did begin to acquire numbers of horses, by the late eighteenth century, they were tough pony stock, probably originally left by friendly passing travellers. In their battles to repel the invading colonists in the 1750s, however, most of the Indians were still fighting on foot. The young George Washington, in charge of the defence of Winchester, described the Indian method of attack:

'However absurd it may appear, it is neverthe-

In the enemy country (*Indian War Party*) *by Charles M Russell.*

less certain that 500 Indians have it more in their power to annoy the inhabitants, than ten times their number of regulars. Besides, the advantageous way they have of fighting in the woods, their cunning and craft, their activity and patient sufferings are not to be equalled. They prowl about like wolves, and like them do their mischief by stealth. They depend upon their dexterity in hunting, and upon the cattle of the inhabitants for their provisions'.

The War of Independence

The traditions of George Washington's family, his military education, his property holdings and his respect for law made him deprecate the break with England that started the eight-year War of Independence. But the idea that taxation could be imposed without the Colonists' representation was, for him, the greater evil. He faced great problems, however. He was not used to handling large bodies of untrained men. The country had no arsenals, forts, navy, foundries or means of credit. The British Government was an ancient monarchy; it had authority, disciplined forces, a powerful navy, possession of the large towns, and war materials in plenty. Yet it was the very untrained quality of the Americans that was to overthrow the British Army; and in that overthrow, the horse was to prove a significant factor.

The American Colonists were aware that the power amassed against them was considerable; on the other hand, the British Army was beset with difficulties. The English had difficulty in obtaining good horses with which to support their infantry; and they were to find, as the Colonists had found when fighting the Indian, that horses were indispensable. The Colonists were certainly not going to sell horses to their enemy. Transporting horses from Britain was a problem because of the difficulty of keeping the horses alive on the long voyage. Eventually, the army was forced to appropriate horses as and when they could find them.

The Colonists, however, possessed some very fine horses. The Southern states of America, such as Kentucky, were ideal for the breeding and rearing of horses, and there was no shortage; every man needed horses for hauling, for carriages, and for fighting and protecting himself against Indian attacks. The animals were generally bred for speed; their saddles were light and well made, and the horses were trained to cover vast stretches of terrain and to subsist as far as possible upon the land. There was brisk trading in horses, and so highly was the animal valued that horse-stealing was regarded as a capital offence.

In the quality of their knowledge about and ability with horses, the Colonists were superior to their British enemy. The army did not like the guerilla-type tactics that were used against them. Like the natives of Britain who first faced the might of the invading Roman legions, the new Americans came out of the forests. They struck, often at night, with terrifying suddenness; they

were master horsemen and masters of the terrain; the British soldiers saw only glimpses of their shadowy adversaries. Their tactics had been learned from the Indians. The principle was: master the horse and use it in any way possible to defeat your enemy. The more organized and formal the enemy, the more likely were the individualistic tactics of the Colonists to disrupt and disorganize. Washington and his army, together with French mercenaries, did fight pitched battles; but one of the most militarily enervating factors of the American army was their skill as riders, their strange but effective mounted warfare. The British Army's firepower might have been expected to decimate the enemy; but first it had to be seen and, secondly, the British Army's lines of communication and supply stretched back over 4800 km (3000 miles).

The Americans were at home in their big country, where distances were vast and patterns of warfare were foreign to men trained in Euro-

Above *The imperturbable Washington. Although never a general of the highest calibre, with his army of farmers, they overcame one of the most powerful of European armies of that time.*

Above far left *Paul Revere's famous epic ride.*

Below far left *The Americans did fight and win pitched battles such as here at Cowpens but were at their strongest while fighting guerilla warfare, using their knowledge of horses and their country to defeat the British.*

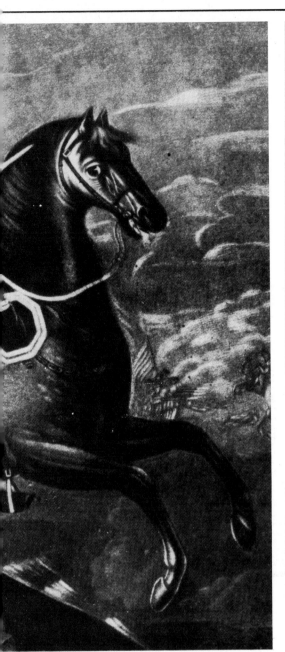

pean techniques quite unfitted for this new theatre of war. Cannon and musket had been thought to presage the end of the cavalry; but in America towards the end of the eighteenth century, the horse was the deciding factor in the kind of warfare employed and in the Colonists' defeat of a better-organized but less adaptable enemy. The war was hard and bitter, and, but for the imperturbable Washington and his army of farmers, the British Army would have triumphed.

Indian tactics

By the early nineteenth century, Indian skill in handling horses was growing. George Caitlin, the painter, went into Indian territory in the 1830s to paint the tribes and depict their way of life. One of his paintings shows Plains Apaches demonstrating their skill of archery while travelling at full gallop: the painted braves are shown riding past large targets, which they have filled with arrows. Such tactics were particularly successful

Top *Charge! The American soldier riding into battle.*

Bottom *For a long time the Indian's traditional weapons were more dangerous and accurate than the white man's.*

against mounted white troops, who found the same problems in fighting the skilful mounted Indians as the Crusaders had found fighting the Turks many centuries before. Despite having no saddles, the Indians seemed to be glued to their animals; and they were far more mobile and incisive in all their attacking movements.

The Indians conducted a war of nerves. First, they would shadow their victims for some miles. Occasionally, the Indian horses would be seen briefly against the skyline; this initial appearance was intended as a threat or portent. Having pursued the enemy in this way for some time, the Indian braves, on their powerful and swift little ponies, would make swift darting attacks. As one soldier wrote later, 'they went so fast they seemed to lie out entirely straight'. Having made their

first attack, they would often retire, as if giving up, only to re-appear a little later with twice as many warriors. Collectively and individually the Indian was a terrifying prospect. Covered in war paint and uttering fearful war cries, he struck terror into the hearts of even trained regular soldiers.

White settlers, travelling into the interior and heading west, were forced to develop their own counter-measures to the highly developed Indian tactics: a single string of wagons was no safe-guard against these marauding attacks. The travellers developed the technique of assembling all their goods and horses inside a circle made by their wagons. In this way, they were in the strongest defensive position to counter any move from any direction.

Civil war

Less than a century after the War of Independence, a different kind of war was to darken the American continent: the American Civil War of 1861–65. In that war, nearly 250,000 young Americans were to die; the old, rural way of life was to be swept away by the first of the great 'modern' wars that not only involved armies in set-piece battles but also laid waste whole states and their populations, their homes and their means of livelihood.

The American Civil War, especially during the first two years, was to make great use of horses for haulage, for reconnaissance and for marauding cavalry encounters. There was little problem in finding horses, as the whole of the American society of that time was founded upon the values of the horse. The ranch system was so organized that the large herds of wild horses everywhere available could be brought under control, broken and used for work. The general standard of horses, bred in the ideal conditions found in great areas of the United States and in the Southern states that chose to secede from the union, was higher than the standard of those to be found in Europe. The method of breaking horses was very skilful and demanded a quality of horsemanship that was unusually high.

Their tradition of horse-breeding, trading and riding was to place the Southern states in a strong position at the outbreak of the war. Most of the men recruited in the Southern states were from the predominantly rural areas; they spent most of their time dealing with horses. A boy usually brought his own horse when he joined up. On being assigned to a regiment, he would learn to ride with others like himself in the cavalry units that were to prove such a scourge to the North. This considerable skill in dealing with horses was accompanied by a spirit of nobility and old-fashioned chivalry among the Southern armies. To them, it was the act of a gentleman to go off to war on horseback as the knights of old had done. These proud latter-day knights were defending the honour of the South, the honour of their homes and families.

By contrast, the Northern administration was forced to buy inferior horse-stock from devious dealers, many of whom were smuggled North by the leaders of the Southern states. Inevitably, the quality of the Southern horses told; although the loss of a horse brought problems. As it had usually been supplied by the recruit himself, replacement was difficult, and it was necessary to send raiding parties out to ensure that supplies of stolen horses continued to be available. There was no question that soldiers from the Southern states could ride practically anything on four legs, while Northern recruits tended to enlist in the infantry, because they had little expertise with horses.

In an age where the destructive power of weapons was growing with every year, the horse was a vulnerable animal. Although still useful, he

Both settler and Indian had, of course, been made more mobile by the horse, and it proved invaluable as a pack animal in those difficult terrains. In times of great hardship, both white man and red man used the horse for food.

As the nineteenth century progressed, the Indian position worsened. Settlement was increasing at an alarming rate, and the men who were in power seemed determined to banish the Indian completely. Andrew Jackson in 1830 got a bill through Congress which ordered all Indians to move west of the Mississippi. The Supreme Court ruled that such a bill was unconstitutional, but Jackson ignored this and the Army was ordered to force the Indians out. It is no wonder that the Indians took their revenge whenever the opportunity presented itself.

Above *General Philip Sheridan, one of the few Union leaders who could be rated against the superior cavalry officers of the South.*
Below *The surrender of the South.*

had to be cared for, protected, used by men of vision. The American Civil War discovered such imaginative cavalry leaders. They were mainly Southerners, although they had often been in the Union army before the outbreak of war. The great exception was the Union cavalry leader, Philip Sheridan. Sheridan received his basic training at West Point Military Academy, and then fought Indians in California and Oregon. After the outbreak of war, he rose quickly to the rank of brigadier general. In 1862, he defeated a Confederate cavalry force that outnumbered him by nearly six to one, at the Battle of Boonville. He won the battle by sending a small band of picked riders to attack the enemy from the rear, while he appeared to attack them face on. The ruse was completely successful. General Ulysses Grant was very well aware of the talent of this cavalry officer; by the time Sheridan was 33, he was in command of the cavalry corps of the Army of Potomac.

Not all the Union men were so expert with horses, however. When President Lincoln was reviewing his troops before his own Commander-in-Chief, General McClellan, a soldier described the occasion as follows:

'I have seldom witnessed a more ludicrous sight than our worthy Chief Magistrate (Lincoln) presented on horseback yesterday. . . . McClellan was beside him, stout, short, and stiffly erect, sitting his horse like a dragoon, and the contrast was perfect. It did seem as though every moment the President's legs would become entangled with those of the horse he rode, and both come down together, while his arms apparently were subject to similar mishaps . . . that arm with which he drew the rein, in its angles and positions resembled the hind leg of a grasshopper—the hand before—the elbow away back over the horse's tail. The removal of his hat before each regiment was also a source of laughter in the style of its execution —the quick trot of the horse making it a feat of some difficulty, while from the same cause, his hold on it, while off, seemed very precarious'.

The Chief Executive was not the only rider to find his horse difficult to handle. One night, during the campaign at Vicksburg in 1863, General Grant had had more than enough to drink—possibly to fortify his spirits. Sylvanus Cadwallader, a correspondent of the *Chicago Times*, pulled off Grant's pants and boots and got him to sleep. The general, however, woke up and demanded more liquor. He staggered from his tent and rode through the camp on his horse, un-

dressed as he was, outdistancing the pursuing Cadwallader, scattering camp fires and angry troops (who fortunately did not recognize the dishevelled figure of their commander). Eventually Cadwallader caught up with the wild horseman and led him back to the camp.

Such humorous incidents were few and far between; the war was bitter and costly, and horses and riders were cut down in swathes in battle after battle. The typical American saddle-horse, developed over a period of over 400 years from English thoroughbreds and crossed with Kentucky saddle-horses of older ancestry, began to be in short supply, and mustangs and other tough little 'cowboy' ponies began to be shipped in from states in the West. There was also direct trade with some groups of Indians who were able to supply large numbers of rideable horses.

Two distinguishing characteristics of Southern cavalry officers were their spontaneity and imagination. Their officers, men like Nathan Bedford Forrest, were untainted by war training or strategy. They chose to fight where their horses could live off the land. They did things simply. They rode fast, they rode far, and when they got down from their horses they were as effective as the best infantrymen from the North. Their abilities were comprehensive; they had learned a great deal from the Indians. They knew how to live lean; how to surprise, how to face hardship and overwhelming odds. Forrest moved horses faster than almost anyone in the whole war. His strategy is reputed to have been contained in his wry aside: 'to git thar fust with the most men'.

Sherman, one of the hardest, most uncompromising soldiers in the Union army, recognized that 'there will never be peace in western Tennessee until Forrest is dead'.

But if Forrest was the wild genius of inspiration, the great master of cavalry strategy and horseman extraordinary was J E B Stuart, the Confederate officer. So incisive and brilliant a tactician was he that 'Stonewall' Jackson declared him a second Murat.

After West Point, Stuart had learned about horsemanship and strategy in fighting first against the Apache Indians, and later against the Cheyenne. It was then that he had met Robert E Lee, with whom he was to fight against the Yankees from the North. General Jackson said of him:

'He is a rare man, wonderfully endowed by nature with the qualities necessary for an officer of light cavalry. Calm, firm, acute, active and

Below *The Battle of Fairoaks showing General Casey's gallant charge to save the guns.*

Custer's last stand. Fighting in ever-decreasing circles the Indians picked off the men and horses until the last white man was dead in one of the Indians' last major stands for their territories.

enterprising. I know of no-one more competent than he to estimate occurrences before him at their true value'.

Although his achievements in pitched battles are justly famous, it is for his remarkable reconnaissance manoeuvres that Stuart is best known. In 1862, when McClellan's army was approaching Richmond, Stuart, with 12,000 horsemen and two cannon, headed north and then east, cutting clean through the Yankee supply lines, destroying their telegraph, smashing their baggage train and capturing over 250 horses, before completing his circular movement back to Richmond.

In October of the same year, he performed his most daring manoeuvre. With a force of 1800 men, he crossed the Potomac and marched by way of Chambersburg. Although encumbered by captured artillery, men and horses, he covered 80 miles (129 km) in 27 hours; and then again forced a passage of the Potomac in the face of superior forces. Besides his many prisoners, Stuart brought back over 1200 valuable captured horses for the Southern cause. President Lincoln wrote in some despair to McClellan: 'Stuart's

cavalry outmarched ours, having certainly done more marked service on the Peninsula, and everywhere since'.

In 1846, in the Wilderness campaign, Stuart received a fatal injury. Ironically, he was leading a group of 80 horsemen in a flanking attack that was routing the Federal forces. As they turned, a Yankee soldier who had been unhorsed and was running from the field, turned and fired the fatal shot as Stuart rode by. So the most noble symbol of Southern chivalry was struck down by the vicissitudes of war. One of his enemies said of him: 'You know I had little love for Stuart and he had just as little for me; but that is the greatest loss the army has sustained, except the death of Jackson'. A year later, Lee had surrendered and America's most terrible war had come to its bloody close.

The 'Indian problem'

After the Civil War, the American cavalry forces, finding little to occupy them, turned their attention increasingly, with encouragement from the Administration, towards attacks on Indian groups.

Sherman and Sheridan, the Union generals, were among the worst offenders in the persecution of the Indians. In 1869, Sherman, having ordered Sheridan to protect the railroad, told him it would help to bring the 'Indian problem' to a final solution.

'I am of the belief that these Indians require to be soundly whipped and the ringleaders in the present troubles hung, their ponies killed and such destruction of their property as will make them very poor', he said. He followed the thought with the deed, by engineering the killing of an old but symbolically powerful Indian, Chief Black Kettle. Sheridan chose one of his officers, George Custer, to assist in his base scheme. Custer had been court-martialled a year before for deserting his post and, ironically, for executing without trial deserters from his own 7th Cavalry. He was, however, to suffer retribution in the Indians' final act of retaliation.

In 1876, General Sherman instructed Sheridan to begin military operations against Indian tribes in the Black Hills, an area given to the Indians in the Treaty of 1868. Chiefs Sitting Bull and Crazy Horse were encamped near the Little Big Horn River in the Dakota plain. After the first 7th Cavalry attack, the Indians, mustering under Chiefs Sitting Bull and Crazy Horse, began to shoot the horses from under the cavalrymen. Then, forming into a pincer movement and attacking on two fronts, the Indians forced the soldiers into a small, tight formation on Battle Ridge.

Surrounded by dead and dying horses, Custer and his 7th Cavalry fought to the last man, picked off one by one by the mounted braves who rode around them in ever-decreasing circles. The Indians, attacked on their ancient holy lands, had replied in the only way the white man understood. In the words of Sitting Bull:

'We did not go out of our own country to kill them; they came to kill us and got killed themselves. The Great Spirit so ordered it.'

Gradually, all the Indians were forced into reservations. Sitting Bull and Crazy Horse, like many other Indian chiefs, died violently. Despite his prodigious skill with horses, and in guerilla warfare, the free Indian had lost; the white man had won.

The Crimea and after-
The changing face of war

After the enormous changes in military techniques, which came to fruition with Napoleon, the years which followed his demise were relatively calm. There had been such enormous losses on all sides in Europe, with ruinous economic consequences, that no one wanted to upset the equilibrium. The Duke of Wellington, who had won fame at Waterloo, was to live for many more years in the long peace that followed. And yet, in the years before the outbreak of the Crimean War, the powers in Europe were to forget the awful lessons of the Napoleonic era.

The Crimean War

Nearly 40 years after the American Civil War, Col. G H Henderson, the military historian and strategist, compiled a list of what he thought to be

The final use for the horse in battle – 'Field Artillery' by H W Koekkoek.

Above *The long winter campaign caught the British army ill-equipped to withstand the appalling rigours.*

Right *The Charge of the Heavy Brigade and its success had a heady effect on the British forces and acted as a curtain-raiser to the ill-fated Charge of the Light Brigade.*

the only successful cavalry manoeuvres carried out in Europe between the time of Napoleon Bonaparte and the end of the nineteenth century. His choice numbered seven, among which was the victory of the British Heavy Brigade at Balaclava, in 1854. France and England had declared war on Russia on the slenderest of pretexts, though ostensibly to assist the Turkish Sultan, who had been unable to prevent Russian forces occupying two of his provinces at the mouth of the Danube.

The whole business of the Crimean War was conducted incompetently. The man in charge, Lord Raglan, a veteran of the Peninsular War, was so old and inclining to senility that he often spoke of the enemy as 'the French'. His seconds-in-command, Lord Cardigan, who commanded the Light Brigade of Cavalry, and his distant cousin, Lord Lucan, who commanded the Heavy Brigade, detested each other. Lucan tended to be slow to act in battle, though he was prepared to live in the same conditions as his men. Cardigan lived on his yacht, which was moored in Balaclava harbour. He became known as the 'Noble Yachtsman'; Lord Lucan became known as 'Lord Look On', because of his dilatory attitude to action.

In making his list of successful cavalry campaigns, Colonel Henderson was indicating the fundamental change that was taking place in the art of warfare. By the very nature of their effect, artillery and firearms had resulted in a change of role for the military horse. It could no longer be used in direct frontal attacks, because it presented such a huge target. Its attacking role would have to be one of speed, and of surprise; often it was most successful in night or early-morning attacks. Its secondary role, which became more important as its attacking role diminished, was in reconnaissance, communications and pack work for supplies and artillery. The old fiery attacking manoeuvre, so beloved of cavalry leaders in the

Above left *D W H Russell, the first 'war' correspondent. It was his reports sent back to England that brought the reality of the war home to the nation.*

Above *Russian and British soldiers alike charge into the conflict.*

seventeenth century, was nevertheless close to the heart of cavalrymen even in mechanized warfare. The romantic concept of the horse, throughout history, was of a dashing steed, plunging to glory in the midst of battle. The Crimean campaign was to provide two examples, one a glorious success, the other a total failure, of just the kind of full frontal attack that would not have been out of place in the seventeenth century.

Conditions at Balaclava

It was surprising that the British were able to achieve anything at all; they lacked organization, and dreadful conditions were suffered by both horses and men. William Russell, war correspondent of *The Times* newspaper, sent back horrendous accounts of the dreadful scenes he was witnessing at the front. Not the least of the evils seen by Russell was the treatment of the English horses:

'Horses drop exhausted on the road and their loads are removed and added to the burdens of the struggling survivors; then after a few efforts to get out of their Slough of Despond, the poor brutes succumb and lie down to die in their graves'.

and later:

'It is really humiliating to our national pride, and distressing to our sense of what we might be, and ought to be, to see the French entering Balaclava with their neat wagons and clean looking men, and stout horses, to aid our wretched-looking, pale weakly soldiers and emaciated horses in carrying up ammunition'.

It is a measure of the dreadful quality of the British planning, that the army should have appeared so ineffectual; the Russians were not master cavalrymen, nor had they superior horses. Although it has been estimated that there were over 30 million horses in Russia before the Revolution, they were not, generally speaking, of a high quality. Though many were of a strong and powerful frame, they lacked the traditional training and finesse, seen especially in horses from the Hautes Ecoles, that distinguished the truly capable and exciting cavalry horses. It was probably this lack of collective spirit that allowed the success of the Heavy Brigade at Balaclava against almost insuperable Russian odds.

Because of the frequent differences of opinion between Lords Raglan and Lucan, there were few horse reconnaissance movements during the whole of the Crimean War. The resultant lack of knowledge about the enemy position caused the Battle of Balaclava in October 1854. Three days before the battle, a false alarm had meant a large number of infantry and cavalry being prepared and having to stand ready in the bitter cold of a Crimean night. During that night, the commander of that famous group of horsemen, the 17th Lancers, died from exposure to the bitter weather. Consequently, when a message was received of a Russian attack, there was little haste used in preparation.

The Charge of the Heavy Brigade

Eventually, Lord Lucan led the Heavy Brigade into the southernmost of two valleys dividing the plain at Balaclava. He proceeded to a position that placed him beneath a ridge occupied by the Russian army. There, he received a number of strangely worded orders from the ancient Lord Raglan; orders that confused rather than directed.

The scene was set: English, French and Russian troops all positioned, as it were, looking down into a shallow amphitheatre where the British Heavy Horse Brigade was about to en-

Above *The Charge of the Light Brigade from the film of the same title.*

Far left *The Battle of the Alma showing the decisive Charge of the Heavy Brigade.*

Centre left *The return from the Battle of Inkerman.*

Left *'Elegant, high-handed and querulous', Lord Cardigan, commander of the Light Brigade.*

Below *The disastrous charge of the Light Brigade showed the futility of pitting the horse against the full tirade of cannon.*

counter a charge down the slope by about 5000 Russian cavalry. The Russian line was about three times wider and deeper than the 300 British horsemen. Down came the lances into the attack position, the thunder of hooves thrown back from the rock walls of the valley as they built the charge down the slope. To the amazement of all observers, Brigadier-General Scarlett· drove his Heavy Brigade in arrow formation, straight at the centre of the Russian advance. It was a most extraordinary, gallant manoeuvre.

The Russians broke over the red ranks of the Scot's Greys, the Inniskillings, and the 4th and 5th Dragoon Guards. There was the terrifying clash of steel, the cry of horses, the battle trumpet heard among the flashing steel, as the Heavy Brigade fused with the Russian masses. Shouts and trumpet calls reverberated from the rocky walls. Somehow, the British Brigade, shattered and torn, continued through the Russian ranks, breaking and turning their impetus. Seen from the heights, the whole battle was as if witnessed in slow motion. The huge, grey bulk of the Russian cavalry force was thrown off-centre,

wrenched askew; a small knot of Russian horsemen turned back the way they had come; the charge was broken. Turned by the fiery daring of Scarlett and his incredible horsemen, more and more Russians forsook the place and charged in confusion for the heights they had recently so scornfully left. Scarlett, his uniform in ribbons, and bleeding from sabre cuts, led his men back out of that rocky place, after one of the most audacious and gallant cavalry attacks in the history of the British Army. It was the first time he had seen action.

Instead, then, of urging his reserves to continue to harass the Russians, Lucan gave no such order; Cardigan, too, in charge of the Light Brigade, did nothing to continue the decimation of the fleeing Russian horsemen. It was an error to be paid for in full, when the Light Brigade, in turn, made their famous and foolish attack. Left, however, at the scene of the clash was the inevitable and dreadful tableau of the dead and dying. Horses, their flanks suffused with blood, their eyes white with fear, their legs kicking, their hocks cut to the bone, struggled to rise to their feet. Men lay upon men, Russian and English tangled in death. The terrible price for the most superficial result could be seen there before the eyes of the assembled armies. Is it any wonder how effective the graphic despatches of William Russell were when they were received back in England? One of his most poignant descriptions tells us:

'There is now on duty in Balaclava a party of orderlies, whose duty it is to go about and bury all offal and dead animals every day. On an average they have to inter the bodies of twelve horses each twenty-four hours, all of which have died within the town'.

Such was the inevitable end for the proud-trained animal that took his place in the cavalry line before each battle; instead of the occasional moment of glory, his reward was to become stinking offal, rotting on some obscure battlefield.

The Charge of the Light Brigade

Perhaps the most extraordinary example of in-competence and stupidity to be found in the whole war was the tragic attack known as The Charge of the Light Brigade. This singular act of folly has become part of the fabric of English myth and legend, thanks to the poem written by Lord Tennyson.

The ambiguity of the messages sent by Lord Raglan to Lord Lucan was based upon the different positions that both men occupied at Balaclava. Whereas Raglan was situated on the heights, Lucan was lower down, on the plains, with the 600 men of the Light Brigade of Cavalry drawn up in ranks.

Having seen the Russians advancing, apparently with the intention of capturing guns left by retreating Turkish gunners, Raglan sent a message purporting to ask the cavalry to advance. Lucan, who could see nothing on the plains, appeared to sit upon his horse doing nothing. Raglan could see both sets of men and he became angry at Lucan's inactivity and sent him another message advising him to get the cavalry to move at once. The message was given to a Captain Nolan, with the added oral advice to tell Lord Lucan that the cavalry were to attack immediately.

Captain Nolan was an impetuous man; moreover, he was the kind of cavalryman who acted first and thought about it afterwards. He had seen service in India and was a typical product of the army riding schools. He had all the zeal of a man brought up in the glorious traditions of the cavalry, believing in particular that the Light Brigade could perform any feat, however dangerous, provided always that the action was carried out with spirit and flair.

Upon receiving Raglan's message, Captain Nolan spurred his horse furiously down from the heights to carry the note to Lord Lucan. When Lucan received the message to attack, he still did not know in what direction or even whom he was to attack. Nolan proceeded to inform Lord Lucan that Lord Raglan had categorically ordered an immediate attack. Lucan decided to order Cardigan and the Light Brigade to make a frontal attack on the Russian Army and their gun em-

Below *The highly disciplined Prussian troops, a legacy from Frederick II, in the centre of Paris, at the end of the Franco-Prussian War.*

Below right *One of the most unsavory and distressing aspects of warfare —shooting the wounded horses.*

Above *Charging into battle at Vionville in 1870. In no way could the horse face up to the modern type of warfare.*

placements at the end of the south valley. It was a suicidal order.

Nolan asked a friend in the 17th Lancers if he could join the attack, and was given permission to do so. Cardigan led the men forward seated; he was on his favourite bay charger, called Ronald. They moved slowly at first, but then more quickly as cannon shell burst among the speeding ranks. One of the hussars present wrote graphically of that moment: 'Gripping my sabre which I had fastened to my wrist with a twisted silk hankerchief, I was a moment paralyzed, but the snorting of the horse, the wild headlong gallop, the sight of the Russians before us, becoming more and more distinct, and the first horrible discharge with its still more horrible effects came upon us, and emptied saddles all about me'.

Gradually, with trumpets sounding and weapon glinting, their pace increased until the whole 600 swept down like avengers upon the massed Russians. The Russians could scarcely believe anyone would be so foolhardy; but they were witnessing it with their own eyes.

At about that point of the charge, Nolan burst from the ranks and, waving his sabre, rode diagonally across the line taken by Cardigan, who was leading the attack. Whatever Nolan's reason, it would never be known; he was blown to pieces by a direct hit from a Russian shell. The brigade drove on toward the booming guns and the entrenched infantry.

It is truly miraculous that anyone survived such an assault, but some of them, including Cardigan, actually reached the guns and beyond,

before regrouping and returning through the smoke and dust to where Lucan was positioned. Of 600 men who had ridden into that holocaust, 200 returned. Four hundred horses and men were torn and shattered in that reeking valley, their equipment scattered around, pennants, hats, sabres; and over all was heard the pitiful cry of dying horses.

Such folly roused the whole British nation to complain, and the outcry was appeased only by the return of Lord Palmerston to power and the quick cessation of hostilities. The military horse had made perhaps his final traditional impact upon the progress of a war, in those two famous attacks at Balaclava.

War since the Crimea

After the Crimean campaign, as the fire-power of weapons became more devastating, horses were used less and less for cavalry charges; unless, that is, they were used against dispirited or disordered troops, especially infantry, moving back in a state of panic. Nevertheless, horses continued to be used in great numbers by various countries in war. Their role, however, became one more of ancillary aid than of front-line battle-winner.

The Franco-Prussian War of 1870–71 was one in which the limitations of the old use of horses in battle were shown to have very great consequences. Both armies had large bodies of cavalry, on which they depended. The cost of maintaining horses, equipment, farriers and veterinary officers, however, was high in terms of the apparent little gain; it is now surprising that the military experts began to consider how they might use horses in other ways. The French, in that war, had about 40,000 cavalry members of one sort or another. The German cavalry mustered close to 60,000 members.

The French horses were trained principally in cavalry schools, while the horses of many of the officers were trained in Cadre Noir. At the French school of Saumur, the Cadre Noir formed an academy of horsemanship, which studied the history of equestrian art and everything connected with it. It sought to encourage those special French qualities of horsemanship that went back to the time of Louis XIV; qualities of elegance, panache and precision.

The Germans were efficient, organized, disciplined; already manifesting that consciousness of German supremacy on which Bismarck, the Kaiser and Hitler were to build such terrifying war machines. Their patrol and reconnaissance work was of the highest order; at Vionville, where the French were gaining the upper hand, the German commander set on a cavalry charge such as was seen at the Battle of Balaclava. Despite terrible losses, the German cavalry burst through heavy French gun emplacements, routing the cavalry on the way with their heavier horses and dense marshalling. It was the boldest and most effective cavalry move of the war but one that marked the increasing vulnerability of the horse.

The Franco-Prussian war, at a time when more emphasis was being placed on training, ironically saw the horse being increasingly used as a pack animal.

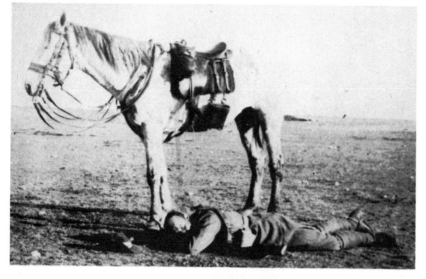

Guerilla tactics: the Boer War

The Boer War, fought between the British and the South African Boer farmers between 1899 and 1902, was in many ways analogous to the American War of Independence. Here, too, a small colony of men, tough, fit, expert in horsemanship and survival, achieved a guerilla-style supremacy over the traditional army of a huge imperial power.

The Boers rode small, sturdy ponies that were accustomed to covering long distances with little effort and with little need for food. Normally moving at a fast walking pace, carrying heavy baggage, the ponies were capable of travelling up to 64–80 km (40–50 miles) a day. Each group of men had their own system of operation. They would cover about 10 km (6 miles) in an hour, and then off-load the ponies and allow them to roll and rest for about 10 minutes, including grazing time, before mounting up and continuing for another hour; and so on. The ponies were taught to stand quietly, unhitched, when an emergency presented itself. The Boers were also very accurate marksmen, and fine judges of land on which to fight.

The British, by comparison, were desultory in their methods. They were not fighting for their lives and lands. Very often, the horses they used were of poor quality, being unfitted for the special conditions on the African veldt and often sickly after the long sea voyage from England. Possibly the only cavalry leader of any note to emerge from the British ranks was General French, who was eventually to relieve the town of Kimberley. He observed the method of fighting used by the Boers and learned from them. It was he who husbanded the qualities of the English horses, in order to make them the equal of the fantastic Boer ponies. It was not until the British concentrated on building up a strong force of cavalry on good-quality animals that they were able to drive the Boers into submission.

The advent of total warfare

In 1903, Lord Roberts, Commander-in-Chief

Above far left *In the Boer War, guerilla warfare was paramount and therefore horses, for a short period at least, regained their ascendancy. The Boer horses, although not superior in breeding, were well suited to the conditions and were well-trained. Here one waits patiently for his master.*

Centre far left *In contrast to the Boer ponies the imported English horses were not conditioned to the climate and terrain of the Veldt.*

Above left *A Boer commando. Tough and deadly accurate with their guns, these farmers fought for their lands with dedication against one of the strongest nations in the world.*

Below left *It was not until the British Army left behind their doctrines learnt from the army manual and emulated the Boers that the war turned eventually and finally in their favour.*

Above *German mounted troops during the First World War. No match for the increasingly efficient armaments, the horse was soon to disappear from the pitched battle of European warfare.*

The long and bloody struggle for Ypres resolved few problems in a mainly static war. Here one of the few positive moves of the campaign as the Germans take over St Julien.

Above *The course of the war virtually precluded any role of the horse other than as a pack horse. Here at the battle of Pilcken Ridge in 1917 a horse is loaded with wiring staples. Fixed to his nose band is the precautionary gas mask.*

Right *Waiting to unload a German munitions train.*

after the Boer War, called a conference of cavalry officers to decide on what changes in strategy might be used by cavalry units as a result of the new developments in army tactics and the greater sophistication of weapons. The experience gained by commanders in the Boer War was to prove very useful in the conflagration that was to envelop Europe in 1914.

The 1914–18 War was a war of attrition. Strung on either side of a line stretching from Switzerland to the sea, the two armies became buried in the impotence of outdated strategies. How the cavalry must have longed for an old-fashioned opportunity of a dash at the enemy! But with trenches, with barbed wire, with man-made swamps, and the dreadful power of machine-gun and shell, the horse seemed to most observers to be an anachronism.

As stalemate gradually extended on all sides, however, there came a great demand for horses from the artillery. Not only did they need large numbers of horses for draught work, especially for field ambulances, but they also needed hundreds of pack-horses. Artillery was the principal weapon of attack, and as the guns became bigger and heavier, so the problem of moving them became greater. The problem was exacerbated by the lack of roads and the terrible state of the camps in which the soldiers existed.

All ammunition was carried to the gun emplacements on pack-horses. The terrible conditions of those pack-horses can be seen in contemporary photographs and films. There was a terrible wastage of animals. Most of the time, they were picking their way over muddy ground spaced between great pools, dug out by high explosives and filled by rain; pools deep enough for horses to drown in. The continual whistle and explosion of shells, the tearing of shrapnel and the stutter of machine-guns all combined to confuse and madden the horses. Never had men and horses been required to perform in such a wilderness, in such a hell on earth.

Sir Frederick Hobday, a famous veterinary

surgeon working in France in the middle of the war years, recorded that, in the space of one year, over 120,000 horses were treated for wounds and disease. Before 1914, the British Army had just over 20,000 horses; during the first three years of the war, it was necessary to purchase over 1,000,000 animals, to maintain some kind of activity in the glue-like mud that bogged down everyone and everything in the shattered fields of France.

At the Battle of Amiens in 1918, the extraordinary experiment of sending three cavalry divisions and three brigades of tanks into action together was tried. It was a futile manoeuvre; they got in each other's way and their special techniques were of no avail to each other. The cavalry did, to a certain extent, mop up units badly mauled by the lumbering tanks, but the horses' need for food and water necessitated an early return to their base position.

The lessons of the war were clear: the days of the military horse were numbered. Ironically, in

Top *Rugged up carefully the horses were usually kept behind the main lines. Veterinary services were provided but often not adequate.*

Above *The soft ground meant that horses were the only feasible method of transporting guns and supplies.*

our own time, the same might be said of men. Cavalry techniques developed over centuries had been proved ineffectual in the first terrible example of total war. The horse had become a dumb beast of burden, its former glory largely gone.

The deficiencies of machine war

In the Second World War, the use of horses was limited to those parts of the world where the topography of the land was such that mechanized transport was not able to be used. Examples are to be found in Malaya, where jungle fighting required the use of large numbers of pack animals; at Bataan, where the Americans were so desperate for food that they were reduced to eating their horses; and in Russia, where conditions were so grim, where primitive roads, frost, swamp and dust halted one of the finest mechanized armies in the world, and where the horse once again proved his worth when all else had failed the warring men.

It must, in the final analysis, be significant that when Hitler's Panzer divisions had reached Moscow, not all the miracles of modern science could prevent the machines from freezing solid; and, in their counter-attacks, the Russian troops, dressed all in white, many of them brought from Siberia, swept down, silent on their sturdy horses (the only effective means of moving), upon the German invaders to drive them back, ultimately to Berlin itself. Indeed, the Germans themselves were forced to use horses in order to make any semblance of movement. And when they were starving, they, too, were reduced to eating their horses.

One of the truly memorable stories of the war concerns a band of Polish heroes, who refused to give up the impossible struggle when Poland had been overrun. Led by a man of indomitable courage, the little band of 300 guerillas, all of them mounted, proceeded to engage in just the kind of noble cavalry tactics that had been known for generations. Using cover whenever they could, they proceeded to harass the invaders on every occasion; until, finally, the patriotic Poles were wiped out and their leader executed. It was a last symbolic fling of the horse in battle in the depressing context of total world war.

The Russian campaign of the Second World War showed the unreliability of machine warfare. Both Russian and German alike found the machine deficient in the harsh conditions and found the horse a worthwhile ally.

The eclipse of the military horse

For thousands of years, the horse has aided man in his perpetual struggle against the changing fortunes of life. For thousands of years, too, as man had indulged his warlike tendencies, the unfortunate horse has been man's speed, strength and salvation. But, gradually, as techniques of warfare became more sophisticated, man found himself obliged to train the horse to overcome, first, its natural fear and, secondly, its natural disinclination to carry a man upon its back. Training methods have in themselves sometimes resulted in the horse's being forced to change its miltary role entirely, in order to continue to be successful.

The changes, taking place over hundreds of years, have usually been changes of degree. The prime reason for using horses has always been that they proved themselves, in all kinds of conditions and in all kinds of role, to be most effective. For the Greeks and Romans, it was as chariot horses; for the Turks, as animals of incredible swiftness, beauty and manoeuvrability; for the horsemen of the Middle Ages, they had to be like armoured tanks, and, for the set-piece wars of the seventeenth and eighteenth centuries, they became, collectively, a unit of power, shock and pursuit. As the twentieth century has unfolded, the residual effectiveness of horses in a total war context has faded. War has become a desperate science, a psychological struggle, in which an electronic circuit is more effective than all the horses ever used by man in the wars or engagements that have taken place since time began.

Yet, because of its particular excellence, the horse still has a place in our military affairs. New discoveries are making any kind of total or global conflict more remote, and so, ironically, man is turning more and more to the contained war; the small-scale eruption that allows countries the luxury of indulging their mistakes without destroying the earth in the process.

Horses are still used all over the world in a military context; principally in situations where the terrain is too difficult to allow machines to make their way. A good example of this is the defeat of the French Army, at Dien Bien Phu, by an enemy whose tactics were those of the mounted bandits, such as existed in medieval Japan. In the final battle, the guerillas moved large amount of artillery in pieces, on the backs of horses, to unassailable positions. The same thing happened when the Americans were fighting in Vietnam. Their elusive and rarely seen enemy made great use of horse transport to bring supplies through dense jungle where no machine could go. Machines do not have the adaptability of horses. In this respect, the horse will never be really eclipsed. The unwillingness of the North American cowboy to give up his steed for a car or a tractor perhaps demonstrates that quality of spiritual affinity between a man and his horse which has been a significant factor in the history of warfare. It is true that the best commanders in war have often been men who had a special regard for horses; a regard for their effectiveness, their nobility, and their willingness to face the very worst conditions to serve their masters.

This spirit of the finest traditions of the famous horse brigades lingers in the ceremonial regiments, which still regularly revive, for the people of Britain at least, the heritage that made the country great. The colour, the pomp, the majesty, the

Right *An exercise called 'Croupade' by the Cadre Noir.* **Below** *Tent pegging by the Military Police.*

Above *The King's Troop appear on the Queen's Official Birthday Celebrations and at the Royal Tournament held in London every year, making a spectacular ride across the arena with guns in tow, recapturing the horses's former glory.*

distinctive flavour of history is evoked by present-day military ceremonial. The splendour of the accoutrements of the horse symbolizes the quality of its pageantry. The Bible speaks of the war-horse and in the most glowing of language, stressing always its power, its beauty and its speed. Great writers have chosen to express their patriotic fervour by describing the feats of the military horse, and poets have immortalized individual horses and individual victories. Ceremonial horses still have this extraordinarily evocative quality; they still excite by their presence and draw admiration for their elegance, beauty and spirit.

At one time, the military demands of the nation defined the quality of the horses being bred and trained; and all too often their fate lay on some obscure battlefield. Today, while ensuring that standards previously set by the military horse continue to be maintained, the great knowledge of horses is being directed towards peaceful ends.

Picture Research: Kay Macqueen